Be a Top Leader!
You Don't Need To Be A Genius!

I0041578

Sixty Nine
Management Tips
For Top Leaders

Samuel L. Dunn

EMETH PRESS
www.emethpress.com

Sixty Nine Management Tips
for Top Leaders

(ISBN 9781609470999)

Library of Congress Control Number: 2016944560

Library of Congress Cataloging-in-Publication Data

Names: Dunn, Samuel L., author.
Title: Sixty nine management tips for top leaders / Samuel L. Dunn.
Description: Lexington : Emeth Press, 2016.
Identifiers: LCCN 2016022181 | ISBN 9781609470999 (alk. paper)
Subjects: LCSH: Leadership. | Management.
Classification: LCC HD57.7 .D84866 2016 | DDC 658.4/092--dc23
LC record available at https://lccn.loc.gov/2016022181

Contents

Chapter 5. The Challenge of the Future / 89

The Author / 101

Dedicated to My Father,

Floyd Beveridge Dunn.

Introduction

Dunn is a businessman who has worked in education for most of his career. His career in leadership and management in universities spans a quarter of a century. Also, during those years he taught graduate level management courses that integrated various business disciplines.

Over the years Dunn wrote many essays expressing his take on various business topics. Many of those essays were given to students who provided their critiques on the topic at hand. The students were typically ones with significant management experience who could add their real-life perspective to the topic. These essays have been edited to form the heart of this book.

The essays reflect Dunn's philosophy of leadership, management, work, and ethics, mostly influenced by his father and by his management experiences. His father was a workaholic. He majored in Latin in college and loved words. In many dinner conversations he would talk about some word and its etymology. He impressed Dunn with the need to study and work hard, give a full day's work to his employer, and work with the strictest ethics. One of his favorite sayings came from the Bible: You reap what you sow. Every action has consequences and the possible results of your actions must be considered before you act. This book is dedicated to him, Floyd Beveridge Dunn.

A big theme throughout these essays is leadership responsibility. Many companies have problems because the board or leaders do not step up to the plate and take responsibility for a problem. They let the problem fester and hope it will go away. When it doesn't go away and things get really bad, then the leaders will act, but often it is too late and significant damage is done.

Best wishes as you read these essays. May they be a stimulus for thought and conversation, and may they help you be a better leader and citizen.

Chapter 1

Strategic Leadership

We Need Leaders

A leader is someone who is able to bring people and resources together and cause them to work toward a stated end. A leader creates goals and culture which together promote goal fulfillment. A leader sets and interprets a vision which improves the status of the organization and the wellbeing of the people involved. A leader takes appropriate risks on behalf of the organization being led.

Are you a leader? Would the people you work with describe you as a leader?

There are scads of workers, many managers, and few leaders. Many people who have been appointed to positions of leadership do not exercise leadership, because they are really managers. Managers are people who use the tools of an organization to help it perform its mission. These are people who can churn out the goods, can make the train run on time, can keep the employees meeting their targets, and keep everybody safe and happy. If that's all they do, they are managers, not leaders.

There are leaders who are not managers. These people can strike a vision, sell it to people and get them energized to move ahead toward a goal, but they get bogged down with the day-to-day tasks needed to make the organization run. These sorts of people often make their colleagues frustrated and mad, because they generate energy which is not channeled in a productive manner.

Actually, organizations need both leaders and managers. Seldom is a person very strong at both assignments. If the CEO is a leader, she may need to surround herself with managers who can put the train on the track and make it go. It doesn't work so well the other way around. If the CEO is a manager and surrounds herself with leaders, those leaders may get frustrated trying to get the CEO to move in new directions.

The jury is still out whether leaders are born or made. It appears it takes a certain personality type to be a leader. Leaders need to be self-confident and risk takers. They don't care so much what other people think of them. They are willing to move into new arenas of work and sometimes even bet the company on a particular direction.

One of the best ways of learning leadership is to study leaders. Also, if you can follow a mentor around, or get a leadership internship, you can learn many leadership skills. Next best is to read about leaders, their ups and downs, and what made them succeed.

On the other hand, it appears that managerial skills can more easily be acquired. There is now plenty of proven research to help managers diagnose company problems and suggest solutions. The manager can implement those solutions and move the company ahead.

If you are heading toward company leadership, one career path is to get yourself appointed as manager of a significant section of the firm. Perfect the skills needed to direct the section; watch and emulate strong leaders; then, go for the golden ring yourself.

Do You Have the Guts to be A Leader?

True leadership takes guts. Leadership takes hard work and tenacity. Leadership means long working hours. Do you really want to be a leader?

Leadership may mean leaving some of your friends behind. If you are promoted to leadership some colleagues that you have worked closely with for years will have to be left behind to continue their work while you go on to new heights. Some of your best friends may become your critics. Do you have the personality to take the loss?[1]

Leaders have to make choices, and many times you won't be able to share the reasoning behind the choices. You'll be criticized for the choice you made, and you'll be criticized for the manner in which you made it. Can your personality stand up under the constant critical bombardment?

As a leader you will have to make personnel decisions. You have to hire and fire. Can you fire a person, if needed? What happens if you need to move your best friend out? Will you find yourself lying awake night after night, worrying about the hard personnel decisions you have to make? Can you take it?

---

[1]Resources: Maxwell, J. (2007). *The 21 Irrefutable Laws of Leadership*. Thomas Nelson

The higher you move up in the organization, the more leadership responsibility you take, the more susceptible you are to public criticism. What happens when your name gets into the newspaper with a negative report? What happens when politicians go after you and your firm? Can you take it?

There's an old saying about leaders: Friends come and go, but enemies accumulate. As you stay longer in your position the number of people who have been negatively impacted by your decisions will increase, and you may find yourself increasingly isolated from the other leaders and the firm's workforce. Can you take it?

Much of this sounds negative, and it is. But if you can take it, being a leader is one of the most rewarding jobs to have. You have an opportunity to improve society. You have an opportunity to be an entrepreneur. You may bring new products and services to the marketplace. You can help many people advance in their careers. At the more personal level, you may have more opportunities for travel. You will have opportunities to help your family improve its lot. And don't forget the increased compensation. All in all, if you can take it, go for it. Become a leader.[2]

Do You Really Want that Promotion?

Gomez was a civil engineer working for a large architectural firm. He had been there for ten years and was doing quite well in his work. His wages were decent and supported his family and lifestyle. The work was white collar and Gomez' output was respected. Then an engineering management position came available at the firm, Gomez applied, and was appointed manager over 12 engineers. His compensation went up 30% and Gomez was quite happy with his new situation.

But within six months Gomez was unhappy with his new job. He now spent his time managing the work and the workforce. He especially hated the personnel decisions he had to make. He had to take a lot more work home at night. His management problems worried him and kept him from sleeping well. Further, he now had few opportunities to do his engineering work. Gomez came to the conclusion that he wasn't cut out to be a manager. He decided he just didn't have the personality.

Now he was stuck in the management position. He talked with the CEO and asked if he could go back to his old job, but the CEO said that

---

[2]Samet, E. (2015*). Leadership: Essential Writings by Our Greatest Thinkers.* Norton.

wouldn't be possible. The firm had already hired Gomez' replacement as engineer and didn't need another one. Gomez would have to stick it out or leave the firm.[3]

This wasn't a case of the Peter Principle at work, for Gomez had the smarts and skills to do the job. He just didn't like the new job. Rather than having an enjoyable job as engineer, he now had a job he came to detest.

As happens to many people, Gomez didn't do his homework before taking on the new assignment. He had watched his previous manager and thought the job looked quite interesting and relatively easy. Also, the additional compensation was very attractive. But he didn't do a self-analysis about likes, dislikes, skills, and abilities. He didn't use one or more of the many tools that are now available for self and job analysis. He didn't talk to the outgoing manager about the nature of the job, or talk to people who held similar positions. His failure to self-diagnose and learn more about the new job got him in trouble downstream.

Lesson: New titles and higher compensation may not be what they are cracked up to be.

What Kind of a Decision Maker Are You?

Almost all management decisions of any consequence involve risks. There are risks to the firm, risks to the decision-maker, and risks related to the decision at hand. Leaders vary in their willingness to take risks. Some are risk-adverse and will not be willing to take risks of consequence. Other leaders thrive in taking risks. Some may even be willing to bet the farm on a particular decision.

I worked closely with a fellow who was risk adverse. In thinking about an action he wanted all the details about the action, its implementation, and its potential consequences. I think of him as a 95% decider. He would not move on a proposal unless he knew almost everything about it in detail.

Another person I worked with was a 50% decider. He wanted to have the big picture of the proposal and the major features and principal consequences. He wanted to know some of the details and significant anticipated milestones. He worked with the informal leaders and invited some people to critique his planning. A third person I know was a 30% decider. This third person wanted the big picture, the prin-

---

[3]Resource: Maxwell, J. (2011). *The 5 Levels of Leadership*. Center Street

cipal features, and the upside and downside consequences. His attitude was that the details would be figured out during the implementation phase.

You can imagine that the time to make a decision varied significantly among the three leaders described above. The 95% decider took a long time to make decisions. When he did commit to a direction, the execution was straight-forward and implemented without much heartburn among the staff, for the consequences of the proposed thrust was recognized and taken care of in advance. The 50% decider took a shorter length of time to make decisions than the 95% decider. Whatever details were left to consider were fixed on the run. This approach caused some dissatisfaction among the staff, but generally there was support of the direction.

The 30% decider pulled the trigger on the decisions without a lot of groundwork with the system. As the new thrust was rolled out and problems emerged, he worked to solve the problems and keep the thrust moving in the right direction. This sometimes caused turmoil in the staff and disrupted operations during the implementation stage.

Because of his personality, one could not imagine the 95% decider betting the farm. His strategic planning involved small, incremental goals. His philosophy was business-as-usual. He was willing to take little risks and move the firm ahead in small increments. On the other hand, the 30% decider in his strategic thinking established goals more difficult to reach. He was more conscious of the changes in society and the industry and was willing to make more changes now to get ahead of the challenges.

Just as individuals can exhibit varying decision-making characteristics, teams and boards can also develop risk-taking characteristics. It was my privilege to do some work with a company which had an activist board. The board's personality was one of risk-taking. At the time I observed their work the board had bet the farm on a particular direction for the firm. It was going to take about three years to implement the new thrust. At the end of three years my prediction was the firm would be very successful, or it would go out of business; I didn't see much middle ground. For me it was an exhilarating experience to see the energy the board exhibited and its commitment to the risky future.

Now none of the three approaches is fundamentally wrong, but one approach or other may be more appropriate at a particular time in a firm's history. If the industry or environment are changing rapidly, the decider who is willing to take the most risks may be most appropriate.

If there is not much change in the environment and the competition, the risk-adverse decider may be most appropriate.

The closing question is this: What kind of a decider are you? Have you thought through your decision style? Do you have a team that works well with your style and covers whatever weaknesses your style brings to your firm?

The Big Question: What is Strategic Leadership?

One answer: *Strategic leadership is a mindset.* It is a mindset that looks at all leadership decisions through the eyes of strategy and vision.

Here's the situation. Leaders have to make dozens of decisions each day. Some of them are trivial and don't take much time; some are consequential and take lots of time. Whatever the level and consequence of the decision that must be made, the *strategic* leader always has in the back of her or his mind the questions: How is this decision going to impact the direction of my firm? How is it going to move us along toward meeting our strategic goals/objectives/vi-sion? What can I do now in this decision that will have a positive impact five/ten years from now?[4]

As one moves higher in the firm, the decisions typically become more consequential. Ideally, the less important decisions should be delegated to folks at the lower management levels, leaving only the most important matters to come to the top. These higher level decisions are especially important to the firm's strategy, and the leader must be thinking about the long term impact of each decision.

Unfortunately, sometimes the senior management of the firm is too worried about the quarterly financials and manages in order to make the quarterlies look good. Also unfortunately, decisions that may prop up the quarterly statements may not be the best decisions for the long-term health of the firm. It is better to develop a firm culture that prizes long-term health rather than a short-horizon planning culture.

---

[4]Resource: Pasmore, B. (2015). *Leading Continuous Change: Navigating Churn in the Real World.* Berrett-Koehler.

It is easy for senior leaders to get their eyes off the strategic ball and handle decisions without considering their long-term consequences. It takes a mental and cultural discipline to be a strategic leader.

Responsibility for Strategic Planning

Who is responsible for the strategic plan? Right off we can say that a necessary, but not sufficient, requirement is that the Board of Directors and the CEO must be champions of the strategic plan, or it most likely will fail. The CEO may have had a heavy hand in developing the plan, but if she is not behind the plan, pushing the plan, selling the plan, and managing the plan, the plan will likely fail. Also, if the Board is not on board, the efforts of senior management will be undercut.

The CEO is the PIC (Pilot in Command). It is her responsibility to assure that the plan is carried out. The CEO must have a management structure in place and control and command responsibilities delineated to make sure the plan is carried out.

Responsibility for execution of the various elements of the plan must be assigned to specific individuals, and those persons must have the authority and budgets to carry out the assignment. Specific milestones must be set. Reporting calendars must be developed so that the senior management and especially the CEO are regularly learning about the status of the strategic plan and how or whether it is being executed.

The management culture must be such as to monitor the internal and external environments and provide for alterations in the plans as the situation may dictate. New developments in technology and disruptive technologies, new laws and regulations, and changes in the environment may require broken-field running. Communication channels must be in place to allow quick modification of plans as necessary.

Ultimately, the CEO is the key person in developing and executing the plan. Without his or her support, the plan may become a book on the shelf, to be referred to reverently and otherwise ignored.

Who Develops the Strategic Plan?

In the book *Strategy Safari,* by Mintzberg, Ahlstrand, and Lampel, ten different schools of thought about strategic planning are described.

Each of those schools has its own perspective on development of strategic plans. This book is good reading for anyone serious about strategic planning.[5]

One of the most common ways strategic plans are developed is by company committee. Here's a common approach: The CEO decides the company needs a strategic plan. The firm has six divisions. The CEO appoints one person from each division to sit on the strategic planning committee and charges the committee to come back in six months with a strategic plan for the firm.

Sure enough, six months later the committee coughs up the plan. Most likely it will incorporate the wish list of the six divisions. The report will be a compromise, the least common denominator, of the ideas from the six representatives. Incremental improvements will be delineated for each division. Changes in the environment may be observed, but little is recommended to meet the challenges of the environment. The plan will incorporate a Business as Usual (BAU) model of the future. Some ideas about the future may be incorporated, but the BAU mentality will prevail. No Big Harry Audacious Goals (BHAGs) will be presented. No radical changes. Nothing to grab the imagination and passion of the firm's stakeholders. Nothing to get excited about. Nothing to which you would tie your career, or risk your personal future. No betting the farm. Just BAU. If the plan ever gets executed, life may be incrementally better at the firm, and that's about it.

The problem with this approach is that, generally speaking, strategic planning by company committee doesn't work out all that well in practice. Committee members have too much skin in the game to see the big picture of where the firm might go.

If that is the case, where do good strategic plans come from? That's easy to answer for most firms: from one person, usually the CEO. The CEO should have the big picture in mind and should have a vision of where the firm could go and what it could become. Furthermore, the CEO has the power and budget to make sure the plan gets authorized by the board and is implemented throughout the firm. Probably the CEO is the only person in the firm who can promote and execute a BHAG. The CEO is probably the only person who can take substantive risks.

Examples of visionary CEOs are easy to find. Check out Bill Hewlett and Dave Packard. Bill Gates and Microsoft. Jeff Bezos and Amazon.

---

[5]Resource: Mintzberg, H., Ahlstrand, B., & Lampel, J. (1998). *Strategy Safari*. Prentice Hall Europe.

John Rockefeller and the University of Chicago. John Kennedy putting a man on the moon. Steve Jobs at Apple. These leaders had grand visions that caught the imagination of key stakeholders and led to great achievements. Generally it takes a visionary to develop an outstanding strategic plan, someone who is willing to commit fame and fortune to making the dream come true.

Time Spent on Strategic Leadership

Time spent on strategic leadership varies from firm to firm, depending on many factors. If the firm is stable and doing well, if the industry is stable and environmental factors are beneficial for the firm, then leaders may not need to spend as much time on strategic leadership as do leaders working in disruptive environments.

Regardless, the higher one moves in an organization the more time should be spent on strategic leadership. Senior leaders of a firm should be spending 25% or more of their time with big-picture, strategic issues. This would include time required to sell the firm's vision to its stakeholders. Routine management matters--I call it making the train run on time--should be left to subordinates.

I was in senior management of a division in a firm in which we took long-range management seriously. The three senior leaders of the division spent one day a week in planning discussions. To prevent disruptions we met away from the company site. Some of our best work was done in those eight years when we devoted prime time to planning and long-range thinking. We were able to double the size of the division in terms of income and customers. The planning was quite fun. For us the main challenges did not come from planning, they came from execution of the plans.

How Far Out Should The Planning Horizon Be?

Some have argued that we really can't know the future, and hence planning should be very short term, i.e., the planning horizon is close. Others argue that while we don't know the details of the future, we still have a general idea where our industry is going and the technologies that are likely to be relevant to our industry over the next few years. This latter group would also argue that we know a considerable amount about demographics, such as size and ages of populations and general societal trends such as marriage rates, birth rates, etc. We can also get clues to the future by looking at government policies at the local, state, and national levels.

Futurists talk about business-as-usual (BAU) futures and catastrophic futures. BAU futures planning is built on the assumption that there will be changes but they will be gradually introduced into society. Catastrophic futures planning considers the possibility of a major catastrophe of some kind, such as a nuclear war, or a tsunami that wipes out critical production facilities, or a devastating epidemic, etc.

One measure that has been proposed is that the planning horizon should be at least three business cycles out from now. If there is a change in company direction it will take a cycle or two to modify the current direction while starting to implement the new direction. Hopefully by the third cycle the new company can be starting its implementation of the new direction/products/services. According to the three-cycle measure, if the business cycle is 18 months long, then use a planning horizon of 54 months—four or five years—as the time for your strategic plan.

In higher education the business cycle is usually taken to be three years long. If one is delivering a major in discipline X and the institution decides to drop that major, the institution still has to teach out the students who are currently in the program. Decisions have to be made about the faculty who have been teaching in the program, and many times that means dealing with tenured faculty members. Starting a new program will often take three years by the time the program is developed, gets the approvals of all the internal committees, moves through the administration, on to the board of trustees, and on to the accreditors. Given the three year cycle, many universities develop ten year plans and have a ten year planning horizon.

Military planners working with armament systems have to do very long range planning. It may take 15 years to bring a system from conception, to engineering, to production, and on to deployment.

Some industries have 20 or more years in their planning horizon. A seminar at Boeing showed plans about airplane sales 28 years out. Those sales projections were used as the company developed its financial picture for the future and plans for new planes. At this writing in 2014, Boeing has just announced plans to develop a new plane by 2030.

Strategic Plan Discipline and Creep

It takes discipline to manage a strategic plan. Even if a firm has an outstanding plan and is actively managing it, there are many actions that can cause the firm to move away from its plan, with the result that in a few years the firm is moving in a direction quite different than that originally planned. This may be good or bad.

The firm has to walk a tight-rope. On one hand, the firm needs to have a vision, a direction, and have plans about its desired future. On the other hand, the firm has to be flexible enough to respond to changes in the internal and external environments, changes that might cause the firm to change its goals. Senior managers need to have the discipline to stay the course on one hand, and be open to change on the other.

One way undisciplined firms get in trouble is to let smart people in the firm create new products or services, sell those new ventures to senior leaders, and set the firm chasing the new direction. The new product or service may indeed be something that brings in more revenues, but it may be something that is not congruent with the firm's resources and capabilities. Or, the new thrust may be something that leaders cannot adequately manage. These new activities may take so much management attention that it detracts leaders from their other ongoing responsibilities.

The bottom line is this: Senior management has to be prepared to say no to some good ideas that come along. On the other hand, new ideas *do* come along that need to lead to changes in the firm's direction. Senior management must keep a balance: don't slavishly and blindly stick to a plan, but also don't chase after every good idea that comes down the pike.

One test some firms use to determine whether to move in a new direction is to apply a financial burden test. That is, the firm sets some target percentage, the burden level, and considers new ventures only if that new venture is projected to bring profits at or above the burden level. Suppose the burden is set at 20%. If the firm were to consider three new ventures with projected profits of 15%, 22%, and 18%, the firm would immediately reject the first and third ventures, but would then move ahead to apply other tests to the proposed venture which has an expected profit of 22%.

The burden test applies to the financial aspects of a new venture. But other tests need to be applied to make sure the firm doesn't experience strategy creep. A firm could keep adding more and more products and services, and gradually become so unwieldy that it is hardly manageable. The large number of products and services may confuse the public, distort the brand, lead to less management attention on each segment, and eventually lead to reduced quality, effectiveness, and lowered profits.

A positive action that senior leaders may take with an activity that appears to meet a need, can be done with quality, and meets the financial tests, but doesn't exactly fit the firm, is to spin it off into a new firm. Then the new activity and firm won't detract from the original firm's vision, plans, and brand.

In summary, firms must work to protect their plans, but must also be open to changes that will enhance the firm with its vision, resources, capabilities, and markets.

Know Your Firm

Imagine you are asked to report in five minutes or less the key features of your firm? What topics would you cover?

Here are the 12 things that should be included in such a report.....

1. Name of Corporation
2. Jurisdiction of its headquarters' incorporation
3. Principal products
4. Firm's product delivery locations
5. Gross annual revenues
6. Net net profits
7. Principal customers
8. Principal suppliers
9. Number of employees
10. Principal stakeholders
11. Top Five Challenges
12. Top Five Opportunities

Mission, Vision and Bhags

Does your firm have a mission? How about a vision? How about a mission statement, or a vision statement?

This sounds awfully formal; for thousands of firms the mission and the vision are in the heads of the owner-operator. She knows where the firm is pointed and what it might become. It doesn't make sense to her to write this out in some formal statement. But even if it is not in writing, leaders of small enterprises need to be able to articulate what the firm does and what it intends to be.

On the other hand, as firms grow and the number of stakeholders increase, it becomes important to let the firm's communities know in more formal ways what the firm's understanding of its work is and where the firm is heading in the future. In these cases, formal mission and vision statements can be useful.

Mission and vision are words that have been used in many ways in the past, but one set of definitions seems to be useful. A firm's *mission* is what the firm does, and a firm's *vision* is what it wants to become in the future.

Consider these three mission statements which illustrate different ways of telling what the institution does:

St. Alphonsus Health System. We, Saint Alphonsus Health System, serve together in the spirit of the Gospel as a compassionate and transforming healing presence within our communities. (saintalphonsus.org)

BMW. The BMW Group is the world's leading provider of premium products and premium services for individual mobility. (retailindustry.about.com/od/ retailbestpractices/ig /Company-Mission-Statements) College Church of the Nazarene, Nampa, ID. Our purpose is to know Christ, grow in Christ, serve Christ, and share Christ.

Here are some vision statements from other institutions:

NASA. To reach for new heights and reveal the unknown so that what we do and learn will benefit all humankind. (www.nasa.gov)

General Motors. GM's vision is to be the world leader in transportation products and related services. We will earn our customers' enthusiasm through continuous improvement driven by the integrity, teamwork, and innovation of GM people. (redlac.org)

Albertsons. To be known as the favorite neighborhood food and drug retailer in every market where we do business, with helpful associates, competitive prices and high quality, fresh products. (Albertsons.com)

Northwest Nazarene University. Guided by a vision of the Kingdom of God, Northwest Nazarene University seeks a more excellent way, to be a trans-formative learning community expressing the love of Jesus by forming scholars, nurturing disciples, serving the Church, shaping the culture, re-deeming the world. (nnu.edu)

Going one step further, does your enterprise have a BHAG? A BHAG is a vision on steroids, a Big Harry Audacious Goal. This is a goal so big that the probability of actually achieving it is only about .5. It is a goal that stirs the emotions, that captures the imagination of the stakeholders. It commands attention, drives allocation of resources, and serves as a compelling guide for the organization.

One of the most famous BHAGs was President Kennedy's commitment made in the early 60s that the United States before the end of the decade was going to send a man to the moon and bring him back. Making that happen took the work of thousands of people over many years and billions of dollars, but it happened because of the vision of what might be possible. Know your mission and vision. If you are brave, develop a BHAG.

Values and Core Values

We like to think we have values and principles that guide our lives. We use these principles as guideposts or measuring sticks to help us determine actions to take and thoughts to think. We use these values as ideals we would like to reach and as pictures of what we would like to become. Personal values may not be well articulated, but a trained observer could study each of our lives over a period of time and discern fairly well what our values are.

Companies also have values. A company's values are demonstrated by its actions taken over time. Customers will get to know a company's values and will be supporters or detractors of the company, depending partly on the company's values as they are demonstrated in customer service and Business-to-Business (B2B) behavior.

It's a good exercise to articulate your company's values. What principles guide the company's actions? What does management believe about the work of the firm? How does the firm view its customers? What is the firm committed to do or be?

Many profit and not-for-profit entities publish their values. Here are the values of Northwest Nazarene University of Idaho:

Transformation—We believe education fosters transformation. NNU engages and affects all domains of life—intellectual, social, physical and spiritual—thereby advancing the transformation of the individual, the church and the world.

Truth—We believe education pursues truth. NNU explores knowledge, the wonder of God's creative activity, the story of human civilization and the achievements in the arts, sciences and professions. Ultimately, we believe Jesus is the truth incarnate; therefore, we pursue Christ.

Community—We believe education flourishes in community. NNU provides a learning and faith community that teaches, challenges and encourages each other through intellectual and spiritual practices. Within covenantal relationships we express our love for God and others.

Service—We believe education cultivates service. NNU teaches the importance of a life of servanthood as modeled by Jesus Christ. We learn to lead by giving of ourselves to God and humankind.

General Electric articulates seven values, two of which are:

Passion for our Customers. Measuring our success by that of our customers… always driven by Six Sigma quality and a spirit of innovation

Meritocracy. Creating opportunities for the best people from around the world to grow and live their dreams

Let's drive deeper into thinking about values. There is a hierarchy of values, for some values are more important than others.

A **core value** is a principle that undergirds all you do. It is a principle so important that you would rather die than give it up. Many individuals have a religious belief that is core to them. They would rather give up their lives than give up their faith; they would rather be martyrs than betray the faith.

Companies can have core values as well. The owners of the company would rather close the business than violate their core values.

Toyota claims five core values, one of which is:

Kaizen. Continuous improvement. As no process can ever be declared perfect, there is always room for improvement.

Here's the big question: Do you have any core values? Is there anything for which you are ready to die? Does your firm have any commitments that it would be better to close the firm than give up?

Life Values

Companies have values that should be articulated, and individuals also have values they live by. Unfortunately, many leaders have not taken the time to think through their own values, at least to the point where those values could be articulated and described to others. Have you articulated your values?

Ask yourself these questions: Are there guiding beliefs, philosophies, values that shape my life? Are there principles I can point to that help me make decisions about the important decisions in life? Are there codes of conduct that I use to conduct my life.

To give an example of such a value system, let me show you my statement of values, which I call my Philosophy of Life. These are principles I have embraced for many years. They give me a river channel down which my ship of life sails and helps me avoid the shoals and rocks that might wreck my ship.

Philosophy of Life

Beliefs

I believe: there is one God who is the creator and sustainer of all that exists. Jesus is the Christ, my Savior and Sanctifier. The purpose of my life is to: worship God; continue God's creative work; be God's steward of all that has been entrusted to me; tell the good news about God and Jesus the Christ; and be in service to humanity.

Guiding Principles

In conducting my life and carrying out these purposes, by the grace of God I will live according to the following principles:

Modesty

I will lead a modest and unpretentious life, not ostentatious, but congruent to the responsibility level and the material goods to which I have been entrusted by God. I will not use evil methods to gain power or fame.

Obedience

I will live in obedience to God, the officials of government, my superiors on the job, and in mutual submission to the community of faith. My life will be characterized by strength of character, Christian meekness and tolerance.

Chastity

I will lead a chaste life, one characterized by decency, modesty, purity, and virtue.

Change

I will embrace change in my life and be ready to move as God and the community of faith direct. As the Jesuits say, I will live "with one foot in the air."

Learning

I will be a life-long student. I will always attempt to learn from the Christian Scriptures, the community of faith, from tradition, and from experience. I will make a continuing serious attempt to apply the lessons learned to my everyday life and to my interactions with others.

Service

I will dedicate my life and work to be in service to others. I will work to improve the lot of individuals, and to promote social policy to improve the general society.

Another Take on Core Competencies

Recently some of my acquaintances were listing areas in which their firms had strengths.

A common area of strength mentioned was customer service. It was recognized that if a company does not have excellent customer service the company will have difficulty surviving over the long haul. Every firm must have good customer service. It is expected and necessary. But it is no longer a distinguishing feature. Good customer service is not a core competency.

A strong definition of core competency was given by Hitt, Ireland, and Hoskisson in their book *Strategic Management: Competitiveness & Globalization*. For them a *core competency* is an area in which the company is good and which gives it a competitive advantage over its competitors. "....*core competencies* are capabilities that serve as a source of competitive advantage for a firm over its rivals (p. 362)."[6]

Examples of a core competency would be Wal-Mart's supply chain management system and Caterpillar's technology innovation activities. Given Hitt's strong definition of core competency, good customer service would not typically be a core competency in many firms.

Given Hitt's tight definition, it is sad to say that many companies don't have any core competencies. They may be good in several of their activity areas, but so are their competitors, and there is no apparent competitive advantage. There is no marketable distinctive. A company is lucky to have one core competency. Having two core competencies would be most unusual.

Does your firm have any core competencies?

---

[6]Resource: Hitt, M. A., Ireland, R., & Hoskisson, R. E. (2012). *Strategic Management: Competitiveness and Globalization: Concepts and Cases* (10th Ed.). Independence, KY: Cengage Learning.

Do you have Complimentors? Complementors?

Does anybody like your company? Does your company have any person or any company working for you that is not getting paid by your company? If so, then you have a complimentor or a complementor.

There are many types of *complimenters*. One group may be your stakeholders. These are people or firms that are impacted by your firm and its work and talk positively about you to potential customers. They are complimenters.

Your past customers may be complimenters. The customers you have pleased are willing to tell their friends about your firm and the good work you do. Your suppliers may be complimenters. They may like working with your firm and voluntarily tell others about your work and may tell you about other suppliers that could serve your firm well.

Another class of complimenters, especially prevalent in not-for-profit companies, is the class of volunteers who give of their time and money to help the firm succeed. These are people who believe in the firm's mission and willingly give of themselves to advance that mission. Many not-for-profits could not stay in existence without this type of complimenter.

Many profit and not-for-profit companies have Auxiliaries that exist to support the company. These company-organized and recognized groups provide critical services to the company, most often without substantial cost to the company. Advisory Councils may fit into this category of complimenters as well.

Now let's move *to complementors*, which are different from complimenters. Complementors are entities that set up a symbiotic relationship with your firm and profit by your sales while you profit by their sales. A good example of this type of complementor is the great group of people and firms that write apps for phones and other communication devices. Think of the one million apps available for pads and phones. A phone or pad having a huge selection of apps is going to have better sales, everything else being equal, than phones or pads with few apps. The phone and pad companies may not pay the writers for those apps, but they each profit from the sales of the other.

Another good example of a complementor is the oil industry to the automobile industry. The more cars sold, the more gasoline is sold. These two industries are tied together.

Do you have complimenters? Complementors? Look for them. Embrace and encourage them.

Any Marketable Distinctives?

It has been my privilege over the years to be a university accreditation evaluator. In this work I get to visit other universities and help determine, usually working with a team, whether that university meets its accreditation standards. It has been interesting to learn what those institutions have as strengths and weaknesses and what they tell about themselves in their promotional literature. Also of interest is what the people who work at a particular university say about the university; do they give out the same message the company does in its marketing and advertising?

I've found that many universities and companies like to talk about their competencies, or even their core competencies. In my experience most universities and companies claim more competencies than they really have; even more rare are core competencies. A company is lucky if it has one core competency; two or more would be amazing.

If a company does have a core competency, the next question to consider is whether that competency is marketable. If it is marketable, does it rise to the level of being a marketable distinctive? Webster defines *distinctive* as: "clearly marking a person or a thing as different from others." In other words, how is your company differentiating itself from its competition? It may be a product, a good or service that is different. It may be some part of the company's culture. It may be a brand that has unusual significance. It may be a bundle of goods and services. The thing or things that differentiate your company may be tangible or intangible.

Several questions may help stimulate your thinking about marketable distinctives:

1. Does your firm have any competencies?

2. Does your firm have any core competencies?

3. Are any of your firm's competencies distinctive?

4. Is your firm marketing its distinctive(s)? If so, how? How much of the marketing budget is used to market the distinctive(s)?

5. Is your firm's marketing telling the story why someone would want to buy the firm's product(s)?

6. If you talked to the proverbial person on the street, would he or she be able to say what your firm is known for or known as?

Many companies don't have any distinctives. They just put out their goods and services and compete as an undifferentiated seller; the products sold may be commodities in the marketplace. If that is the case, the company may adopt a low-cost strategy. It works hard to reduce costs and tries to beat the competition on price. If that is your strategy, though, don't expect to get loyalty from your customers. When a competitor is able to provide the same quality goods at a lower price, your customers may very well bolt.

It would be good for your firm to have one or more distinctives, but that is not sufficient. Your firm just *must* be very good at something that the public really want.

Finally, consider whether your firm can develop one of its competencies into a marketable distinctive. For example, is there a critical product that the public wants, one which your firm could become very good at producing and for which your firm could become better known? Then put some focus on that product.

Eyeballs on Customers

Do you really know your customers? Do you know what they like? What don't they like? What irritates them? What delights them? What would they change if they could?

Every company needs to know its customers. Don't be satisfied with having data about your customers somewhere in the company's computer memories. Employees need to know the customers as persons. The CEO and other C-suite people need to know customers.

How can the company do a good job of serving customers unless there is intimate knowledge of those customers? Do you know who your customers are? Are you sure? Maybe your real customer is someone hidden behind a front. Maybe the real deciders about your goods and services are people who are not seen by your salesmen. Don't be satisfied with learning about Echelon 1 customers; dig deep. Identifying your true customer is a first big, good step.

Study your customers in depth. Collect and use data about them. Find out where they live and work. Keep track of contacts with them. Talk to them and ask them what they like and don't like. Find out how, when, and where they use your goods and services. Ask deep questions.

It's important for C-suite leaders to know the firm's customers so the leaders can make informed decisions about firm directions. The leaders must be able to embed knowledge of the customer in their understanding of demographics and social directions.

Kim and Mauborgne in their book *Blue Ocean Strategy* make a strong case for knowing your non-customers as well. Find out why people are *not* buying your products. They argue that the firm should not outsource its investigation into its customers. "A company should never outsource its eyes. There is simply no substitute for seeing for yourself" (p. 90).[7]

Who Is Your Customer?

Old View

In Porter's Five Forces Model, the definition of customer is limited to Echelon 1 buyers. Further, the customer is viewed as a competitor. The customer is not necessarily friendly. Your job is to sell to the buyer at the highest possible price and make as high a profit as possible from your sales. Further, you shop for buyers and sell to the buyer which brings you the most profit. You may enter a bid process with the buyer and give a bid one year and not the next. The relationship with the buyer is short-term and based largely on sales prices.

New View

In the new view, all entities in your supply chain are viewed as your customer, both upstream and downstream. In general, a customer is any entity which influences your profits and whose profits you influence.

The customer is not the enemy, but should be viewed as a friend. The slogan should be: *Get married to your customers.* Most important are the first echelon customers, both upstream and downstream. But many upstream and downstream entities should come under your purview and influence.

Rather than changing vendors and buyers each year with a bid process, select vendors and buyers for long-term relationships. Get acquainted with their needs, their competencies, their profit targets, and help them meet their goals while they help you meet your goals.

---

[7]Resource: Kim, W.C. & Mauborgne, R. (2015). *Blue Ocean Strategy: How to Create Uncontested Market Space and Make the Competition Irrelevant.* Boston, MA: Harvard Business Review Press.

There are several ways you can work with your vendors and buyers. First is product design. Mutually design products to best meet the needs of each. Second, share IT information. Get access to each other's computers and keep track of supply and demand. Together develop supply chain knowledge management (SCKM) and protocols. Together manage conveyance of goods. Put your employees in their plants and their employees in your plants. Mutually develop quality control systems so neither of you has to do much inspection; quality is built in from the beginning. Develop vendor managed inventory (VMI) systems or buyer managed inventory (BMI) systems. Get (and give) access to cost information and help your vendors and suppliers (and you) lower costs.[8]

This new view calls for long-term relationships. You can't change vendors every year, and hopefully you won't be dropping profitable buyers every year.

By using this philosophy you can help your Echelon 1 Vendors and Buyers work with *their* upstream and downstream vendors and buyers and continue the work cooperatively upstream and downstream. Information is shared throughout the entire supply chain.

Integrated supply chains may allow you to have cradle to grave quality control and object management. You may be able to eliminate or reduce bullwhip effects by implementing a demand system from the end customer back to the highest echelon supplier.

Old Story

There is a story about Henry Ford and one of his vendors. The story may be apocryphal. Ford was buying parts for his Model T. He asked one vendor to ship the parts in a box made of wood with a peculiar shape. When Ford received the shipment at the Model T plant, the box was unloaded and the box taken apart. It turned out that a side of the box was the exact shape of a floorboard for the Model T. The vendor was helping Ford reduce his Model T costs. The moral is: Go thou and do likewise for your vendors and buyers.

---

[8]Resource: Porter, M. E. (2008). The five competitive forces that shape strategy. *Harvard Business Review*, January 2008.

Chapter 2

Leadership Decisions

Good Folks, But Inappropriate

Quite often organizations have cultures that do not allow them to easily replace leaders when a change needs to be made. This is more apparent in not-for-profit organizations where the pressure of increasing revenues may not be so critical. The culture prizes loyalty to the mission of the organization. People who have been with the organization for a long time are promoted and left in the new position until things really erode, then those persons are quietly moved on to another slot in the organization or moved out entirely. In the meantime, the organization suffers because of that leader's inability to perform at the level needed.

The culture that allows this to happen is a consequence of a board of directors that is not doing its job very well. This is particularly critical with respect to the work of the CEO. One of the most important jobs a board has is to select the CEO. The CEO must be appropriate for the job. That is, the CEO must have the skills and abilities to lead the organization at that point in time.

A CEO who is appropriate at one time in the organization's history may not be appropriate at another point in time. A competent and appropriate person may be brought in as CEO and may do a wonderful job. However, after some time the organization may be facing a new set of challenges and opportunities that make that CEO inappropriate for the period ahead. It behooves the board to be willing to make a change. The CEO may be "good folks, but inappropriate for now," so make the change.

Another example is the organization that promotes a person heading a $2M division to a top leadership position heading a $50M division. Perhaps the person did a good job heading the smaller division, but doesn't have the skills and abilities to lead the larger division. In that case, the CEO and/or board need to be prepared to quickly move the person out of the $50M division and place him or her where that person's skills match the responsibilities. Or, move that person out of the company entirely. Another way of thinking about this is that a person may be promoted until he or she hits his or her personal lid. Any further promotions will be problematic because the person can't move to the next higher level. Leaving that person in that higher spot may result in that division declining to the level where that leader is effective. Again, the CEO and board must move such people out as soon as possible.

Similarly on down the line of the firm's leaders. The CEO must have a team of leaders who are competent and appropriate for the task before them. If the culture of the firm is such to leave people in place who are inappropriate for the task, then the firm will suffer. The CEO must be willing to make hard decisions with respect to leadership personnel, and put in place people who are competent and appropriate. Don't allow "good folks, but incompetent" to stay in place.

Note that "incompetent" doesn't necessarily mean "bad." These folks may really be good folks. They may have been loyal employees for years who made significant contributions to the organizations. But now the environment has changed, and their skills and abilities are not needed in leadership. If that is the case, make the change and bring in leaders who are both competent and appropriate for the task.

Don't fall into the trap of having a culture that tolerates "GOOD FOLKS, BUT INAPPROPRIATE."

Women in Management

In the early 90s I gave a futurist talk about women in management. I divided management into junior, middle, and senior management. I reported that at that time there was gender parity in junior management, that parity was almost there in middle management, but parity in senior management would take three generations of management (six years each), before parity would be reached. I was so wrong!

It's just about the same now as it was 20 years ago. Parity in junior management, near parity in middle management, and not substantial progress in senior management. It may be accurate to report that 15-20% of senior leaders are women; it varies considerably by industry. It is also accurate to say that senior management and boards of directors are dominated by men.

It is predicted that by 2020 women in the civilian labor force is expected to reach 47 percent. But progress for women in senior management has been slow. The general culture is still largely male dominated, and that permeates business, government, church, education, and military organizations. There is a need for female mentors and models, so as more and more women move into senior management, the percentage of women in management can accelerate. Then there is always the challenge to women of divided interests in careers, families, and kids: dropping out to rear children often sets back career progression.[9]

We leaders need to do everything we can to move women into management. Failure to employ women means that 50% of the brains and ideas are underrepresented. Companies should provide management training and development programs for women. Firms should make sure that women are encouraged to apply for openings and promotions. And critically, firms must assure everyone that women are paid the same as men for similar positions and work.

Have you done a study of the gender distribution of your employees lately? Maybe it's time to review gender distributions by job category, responsibility level, and compensation. If you find women are underpaid or underrepresented, develop plans to correct the inequality.

Let's hope we don't have to wait another 20 years to get parity in senior management.

Avoid Intellectual Incest

Several people in recent days were telling me about hiring practices in their companies. Without exception these informants reported that they tried to hire people that would fit in with the existing company culture. They wanted people who would mesh well with the existing group of employees. Have fun together, work hard together, have the same world view, and even the same politics.[10]

Having a homogeneous culture certainly has some benefits. It is easier to get everybody going the same direction if they have the same perspective and think alike. Lots of arguments are avoided. Antagonistic sub-cultures may be avoided. It may make the bosses' jobs easier.

---

[9]Resource: Hurley, K., & Shumway, P. (2015). Real women, real leaders: Surviving and succeeding in the business world. New York, NY: Wiley.

[10]Resource: Gupta, V. (3/5/2015). Beware of Hiring People Just Like You. *New York Times*, p Bu2.

Acknowledging the advantages, I would argue that having a homogeneous culture is dangerous for the long-term health of the firm. An analogous situation occurs with animal life or plant life. If the gene pool is thin, it is easier for a pest to kill off the entire pool. Also, inbreeding can occur which weakens the strength of the animals or plants.

I argue that having more diversity strengthens the organism, whether the organism be a group of animals, plants, or a firm. Especially important is diversity of ideas about the firm's products or services. There need to be people in the firm who have a different outlook on life, who can challenge the accepted ideas, who look at topics from the perspective of other groups or entities. The firm is better off to have people representing other religions, other races, varying ages. These people working together are more likely to bring in fresh ideas and new products and services. They will contest the status quo.

This is not to argue that we should have in the firm people who are uncivil, who can't get along, who are not politically correct to their fellow workers. People do need to get along, respect each other, and give room for alternate ideas and approaches. Too much uncivil diversity can be a bad thing, just as is too little diversity.

The message here is: encourage diversity in your hiring and in your employees. Provide ways for alternate voices to be heard in the firm and encourage employees to challenge the status quo. With this approach you are more likely to have a firm that can survive and thrive over the long haul and meet the challenges of the environment and market. Avoid intellectual incest.

Execute Your Plan

A high percentage of strategic plans don't get executed. After significant work by the firm's leaders and after high outlays of money and time the plan is adopted, and then often essentially ignored. The plan may be referred to with reverence, but it is left on the shelf to be referenced occasionally when someone needs support for a project, but the plan is, for most practical purposes, disregarded.

Why do so many executives ignore the plan after having worked so hard to develop it? There are many reasons, but, in general, several forces extant in the firm may head off the execution of the plan. The culture is such that the inertia of the business propels it forward without the disruption the plan would create; it is easier to conduct business as usual.

Another significant reason plans are not executed is financial. The new plan calls for new placement of dollar resources. Some leaders will get more funding for their units, some will get less, and some units may go away entirely. It takes much discipline and nerve to move spending allocations around, so it is easier for the CEO and senior management to leave things the way they are.

Another reason plans are not executed relates to personnel. New plans often call for new personnel and separation of some current personnel. Good people who have done a good job may have to find work elsewhere. It is very difficult to separate good people, so it's easier to leave things in place.

Personnel must be assigned to carry out the plan. The activities associated with the plan should be assigned to specific individuals who are held responsible for their activities. Even if personnel are assigned, if they are not given the resources to carry out the assigned duty, then it makes it difficult to see the plan accomplished.

Another reason deals with calendaring and milestones. Planning calendars are not established with firm milestones stating when actions are to be taken and work accomplished. There may not be a reporting system that aggregates the work of the firm with respect to the plan and lets senior management know that the plan is being executed.

It's a big problem if the Board of Directors does not support the plan. If it is a pass through board it may have accepted the CEO's plan in deference to the CEO. The board may not be all that familiar with the plan and may not be willing to put the board's influence behind the plan.

Finally, the CEO may not really support the plan. If the CEO doesn't give the plan her full support and attention, the plan may be doomed.

How does one correct all these inadequacies to get the plan executed? It must start with the board and the CEO. They must buy into the plan, and must be willing to make the hard decisions necessary to move the plan along. Then the CEO and senior management must have the discipline to keep the pressure on to move the organization in the direction of the strategic plan.

Loosen Your Girdle

Many of us moan and complain about the government's intrusion in our daily lives. It seems that everywhere we turn there is a new law or regulation that limits our freedom. What we would like to do is get rid of many, if not most, of those constrictions on our lives. We don't like rules that someone else has made for us to follow.

But before we have a stroke, maybe we ought to look closer to home. What about your company or your family? Are there limits that have been placed on your behavior, limits that seem to be unnecessary, limits that slow down your ability to get real work done? Where did those crazy limits come from? Is it possible you might have put them on yourself?!

We're getting close to the theory of constraints when we talk about the limits we place on ourselves. Here's what sometimes happens. At some point in time we decide it would be good to have a policy to control some aspect of our business, so we make and promulgate the policy. We're happy to have plugged that hole and life goes on. Sometime later we still have the policy, but we don't remember why; the policy has always been there, it seems. The policy may now actually be a drag on our work, because the conditions that caused the policy to be written in the first place no longer exist. But the policy continues on with a life all its own.[11]

So we have constrained ourselves, and the constraint may be so serious that we actually are hurting our business because of some policy, implemented years ago, that causes more work or sets up barriers that we really don't need.[12]

Sometimes managers make a new policy because one or two people have done something the leaders think is bad for business. Rather than deal with the one or two miscreants directly, new rules are developed which tie the hands of all the employees. A shotgun approach to problem resolution is used instead of a rifle.

You may argue that this is just human nature to make new rules and laws; it will always happen. Well, one way we can help ourselves is to write down all our policies, and see what we have created for ourselves. Just converting your policies to written form, away from word-of-mouth distribution, is often revealing. After you know what your policies actually are, then do a formal review and get rid of or modify the policies that are no longer beneficial.

---

[11]Resources: Goldratt, E. (1990). *Theory of Constraints*. Great Bennington, MA: North River Press.

[12]Techt, U. (2015). *Goldratt and the Theory of Constraints: The Quantum Leap in Management*. Dusseldorf, Germany: ibedem Press

A second approach is to put in place a sunset rule whenever you implement a new policy. The policy will eventually die unless explicitly renewed.

Now here's a funny story of a policy that was good, then bad, then good. A church denomination was formed during the Civil War in the United States. The people who started the denomination were mostly from the North. To help fight the war, as an economic boycott against the South, they started opposing the growing and use of tobacco products. After the Civil War ended the people of that denomination continued to oppose the use of tobacco, even though they didn't have a good reason any more. But that policy was part of their tradition and the rule was strictly enforced. Many potential members were lost because of the restriction.

Now move ahead 80 years, to the years following WWII. Evidence started to come forward that using tobacco was bad for one's health. With that new information the denomination picked up the finding and continued to recommend against using tobacco products, but this time as a personal health matter. So history turned in favor of the organization and its continuing policy.

So study your restrictions and get rid of those policies that are no longer helping your organization move toward its strategic goals. Keep the good ones and modify as appropriate as time goes by. Loosen those unneeded girdles that restrict your movement!

One author who has written about the Theory of Constraints is Eliyahu Goldratt. He is the management guru best known for his book *The Goal*.

Job Descriptions

For many years job descriptions (JDs) have been *de rigueur* for businesses in the western world. Employees need to know what they are expected to do, to whom they are to report, and how to go about their work. The JD empowers and provides the limits on what an employee is expected to do. Further, JDs can be used in hiring, for they let prospective hires know what the scope of their duties will be if employed.

JDs can also be used by unions in developing union contracts. They can also be used in litigation that may arise between employee and employer. Further, they can be used to resolve conflict between bosses and employees and among employees.

All these may be good reasons for having JDs, but there is a big downside as well. They may freeze innovation and hinder development of the organization. An employee with a job description may use the JD as a reason for not moving ahead with some innovation that would be useful to the firm. An employee may not resolve a problem because it would be outside that person's JD purview and might trespass on someone else's turf. In a business environment where change comes rapidly, the job descriptions may keep the firm from being agile and responsive to those changes. In effect, the JDs become part of the constraints that impair developments and threaten higher profits.

How JDs act in a particular firm is often determined by the firm's culture. Is the firm innovative? Does it embrace change? Are employees disciplined for overstepping the boundaries of their work? Are innovators prized and rewarded?

If you must have JDs, then there are several moves you can make to help assure the JDs will work in your favor. First, keep the JDs general, not too specific. Make sure there is a clause that allows the JD to be altered at the will of the firm. Make sure the culture is such that innovation is prized and rewarded. Review and update as necessary at least every six months.

Two writers who have considered the downsides of JDs are Edward Lawler III and Christopher Worley in their book *Built to Change*. They argue convincingly for the need of corporate agility in a VUCA (Volatile, Uncertain, Complex, and Ambiguous) environment. JDs get in the way of quick change to the detriment of the firm.[13]

Company Rules

All companies have rules. The rules are part of the life, culture, and DNA of the organization. They give guidance for strategy, for tactics, for daily action. Employees are expected to follow the rules. Employees who disregard the rules are subject to dislike, discipline, and dismissal.

In small companies the rules are often not written down. New employees learn about the rules by talking to people who have experience in the firm and know the lay of the land. The new employee internalizes the rules and gradually starts to conform to the expected behavior.

As companies grow it soon becomes necessary to start to write down the rules, because there are too many rules and many employ-

---

[13]Resource: Lawler, E.E, & Worley, C.G. (2006). *Built to Change: How to Achieve Sustained Organizational Effectiveness.* San Francisco, CA: Jossey-Bass.

ees who need to learn those rules. Employee handbooks are developed and the set of rules gets set into a legal framework to protect the firm, its employees, and customers.

Many companies will have a canon within the canon of rules. That is, there are some rules that are referenced often and are well known in the company. These rules would typically be ones that stipulate ongoing and regular behavior. Other rules are seldom used and few of the employees even know about those rules. These rules are seldom called on to determine action.

What is your attitude toward rules? Do you think rules are laws, and breaking a rule is like committing a felony? Or do you take the attitude that rules are guidelines that direct action when there is need to have a reason for doing something; otherwise ignore them?

Here's my take on rules. First, I stipulate that there are some rules that should be absolutes: these are Class A Rules. For these there are no deviations. For example, *one offense rules* which stipulate that if one person is proven to sexually abuse another; the abuser is dismissed, with no second chance. However, I would also say that there shouldn't be many Class A rules in a company.

Most rules will be Class B rules. These rules tell the normal ways the company does its business. These rules work about 98% of the time. However, there will be exceptions and selected persons must have authority to make an exception. In contemplating an action, the first source to look to for guidance is the rule, and that usually settles the matter. In the instance where an exception is needed, for example to provide better customer service, the employee involved may have the authority to make the exception, or the employee knows who to go to for authorization to make an exception. Most of life is not black and white; there are many grays.

We should regularly examine the rules we do have and update them as needed. Throw out the rules that don't apply any more. Adjust the rules to meet the needs of the environment. [See the essay *Loosen Your Girdle*].

Profit Center and Responsibility Center Management

Profit Center Management (PCM), or Responsibility Center Management (RCM) for non-profits, is a management philosophy that decentralizes budget responsibility to appropriate budget units of a firm. Unit leaders are made responsible for both revenues and expenses of the unit, acting within guidelines and principles established by the firm.

To illustrate, consider a firm that has total revenues A and total expenses E. The firm determined that its principal budget units are: Corporate, Product Units 1-3, HR, and R&D.

After much study, the expenses were broken into six parts and attributed to the budget units as below. Revenues were divided among the three units that bring in revenues. The Product Units are revenue generators, while Corporate, HR and R&D are expense centers with no direct income. Each of these six units has a unit head who is responsible for the budgets of his or her area.

Unit	Revenues	Expenses
Corporate	0	E0
Product Unit 1	R1	E1
Product Unit 2	R2	E2
Product Unit 3	R3	E3
HR	R4	E4
R&D	R5	E5

In budgeting for the next year, the head of Product Unit i is given a revenue target Ri and an expense target Ei, with resulting profit Pi=Ri-Ei, which may be negative. Each expense center is given a target expense number. With no income, each expense center has a negative profit.

The unit head is given considerable freedom in managing his or her budget, and is responsible for both the revenue (if any) and expense side of the budget. For the units producing revenues, if the profit exceeds the targeted profit, that unit can keep a percentage of the excess for approved specials. For expense units, if that unit ends the accounting period with less expenses than budgeted, the unit can keep some of the excess for approved specials. Budget leaders thus may improve the lot of their units if they can increase revenues, or decrease expenses, or both.

Many times in traditional unit management, the heads are given only the expense budget and have no direct responsibility for revenues. It often happens that if a unit comes in under its expense budget, the expense budget will be cut in the following year. Thus budget leaders have incentives to spend all the expense allocation. Under PCM or

RCM, with good incentives built in, unit heads will want to increase revenues and cut expenses.

Many times unit heads are given only an expense budget. This may cause them to focus on expenses, and downplay the revenue side. PCM and RCM cause the unit head to consider the full budget and the interplay between the revenue and expense sides.

Three universities that have adopted RCM are the University of Southern California, Indiana University, and Western Michigan University. Whether your firm is a for-profit or a not-for-profit business, RCM may be the way to go.

Happy With Your Direct Reports?

A colleague of mine is a consultant-guru to a group of business leaders. Recently the guru posed a couple of questions to each of the leaders: When you consider your direct reports, are you happy with their work? Do you have a team that is powerfully advancing the strategic interests of the firm?

Follow up questions are obvious. If you are not satisfied with the contributions of one of your direct reports, why is that person still holding the position? Why not bring in someone who will strongly advance the firm?

Analyzing further, why are you holding on to people who are not doing a great job? Is it a matter of compensation? Are you not willing to pay your reports enough to bring in strong talent? If that is your attitude, have you considered how much the poor performing employee is costing your company? The lesson is, compensate to get the talent you need to make your firm hum.

Is it management overhold? Are you a micromanager and are not willing to give up responsibility to a top mover and shaker, and hence you won't bring in people who won't stand still for your micromanagement?

Is it fear? Are you afraid to bring in a direct report who knows more than you do about her area of responsibility, or someone who has more intellectual firepower than you? Do you get your jollies by knowing everything about the firm?

Is it friendship? Maybe the person who is not up to snuff is one of your close friends. Maybe you brought that person to the company. Maybe the person has been with the firm a long time. Maybe your two families socialize often. Admittedly this is a tough one. But if your friend isn't measuring up, he or she will need to be replaced by someone who can do the job in an excellent way.

In all cases, when you have to let someone go, be sure to treat them well. Give them plenty of kudos for the work they have done. Give them the very best recommendation you can truthfully give. Provide outplacement services. Help them get into another decent job. Try to maintain ties and friendships wherever possible.

If you are the leader, you need to organize for success, and you need to have the very best people helping you move the firm toward its strategic goals. Move the inappropriate people out or to other jobs and bring in people who can most advance the firm.

Are Your Direct Reports Yours?

When you move into a C-level job you will usually have a group of people who report directly to you, your direct reports. They were put into their jobs by the previous occupant of the job, your predecessor. They are now your responsibility.

How are you going to interact with them? Will you get along with them in terms of personality? Are they good at their jobs? Was one or more of them an applicant for your job? Will they respect you? Will you respect them?

You most likely will keep them in their positions for a while, and give yourself a chance to check them out and see how they perform. If they don't perform well, then you may need to let them go into another position in the firm or separate them from the firm. Maybe they perform well, but you can't get along with them; the chemistry is not right, so you let them go.

As time goes by you will bring into those direct reporting positions persons of your own choosing. These people are brought in by you to be part of your team; you have a psychological attachment to the ones you brought in. After all, if they are not up to snuff and you have to let them go, then it may be a reflection of your leadership ability to select the right persons for the job. Those you bring in yourself are part of your team, and you will be assessed partially by the quality of your team.

Then there are the holdovers that are still on the job. What do you do about them? Eventually they will be around long enough for you to assess their value to the firm. You eventually will do a review of each one's work and determine if that person is doing a quality job. If the person survives the review and you determine that the person is valuable to the firm, then you confirm them in the job. Now that person is yours, for you have made a conscious decision to retain him or her in the job. That person is now part of your team.

You may find that the person is not up to snuff, but you believe the person has potential to do a good job and is trainable, so you may stick with the person and buff them up so they will serve you and the firm well.

So over a period of a few months you should have opportunity to put your team in place. Some will be new people you have brought to the firm; others will be holdovers that you have confirmed. You now have a psychological ownership of the entire team and you are partially responsible for their success. Others around the firm will know that you and your team are now fully in place, all cylinders are working, and its full speed ahead. So far as you and your team are concerned, you're ready to conquer the world.

Have You Fired Any Customers Today?

We have often heard the statement that the customer is always right. When we're the customer, we want to think we are always right. But if we are the seller, we shouldn't hold the belief that the customer is always right. Sometimes the customer is wrong. Sometimes the customer is bad, and sometimes we should fire that bad customer.

Good customer service is a goal we should always have. We can even go beyond that and provide service that is a customer delight. We'll always try to do right by our customers. But there are customers that don't do right by us, so we might consider moving those customers on to some other seller.

I like to think of customers as coming in about four categories. First, there are the core customers. These are your customers who love you, who buy in substantial quantities from you, who brag about you to their friends, and don't take advantage of your service policies. You probably make most of your profits from this group. Then there is the great unwashed middle. This is the largest of the four groups. These people are regular customers. They buy, use the product or service in a normal way, and don't eat up your profits by calling on unwarranted service all the time. The third group consists of the poor customers. These folks buy seldom and little and often ditch your product or service after a few trials. The fourth group is the bad group. These folks buy from you, then use up more resources than you made profit.

They call a lot; something seems to go wrong every week. Your service people go out often to correct whatever the problem is. They don't pay their bills on time. Eventually you realize that that customer has chewed up all your profits on that sale.

Once you think you have identified the problem customer, then you need to decide what to do about it. First of all, I'd talk it over with knowledgeable people in your firm. Make sure there is agreement that the customer is a bad apple. Once you have agreement, notify everyone who has contact with that customer, including your phone answering folks, that the customer needs to go away. You still treat that customer in a civil manner, but don't extend any amenities to him, her, or the aggravating firm. Take them off your list to receive company mailings announcing new products or services. Make sure that person doesn't get any more discounts. Start to charge for additional services. Keep the pressure on the bad customer. As time goes by these problematic customers may get the message that you aren't going to kowtow to their whims, and the customers will go away of their own volition. If that doesn't work, you may have to be proactive and just let the customers know that things aren't working out and they should go away. If the customers don't get the message and go way, fire them. Then you will be happier, and maybe even the customers will be happier going to other vendors.

Chapter 3

Advice for Top Leaders

Be Wary Of Success

For those of us who are optimist futurists, having second thoughts about success goes against the grain. If our firm is doing well, revenue is growing, profits are up, the stockholders are happy, other key stakeholders sing our praises, why worry? In fact, things are going so well I think I will take a three week cruise next year instead of my usual one-week cruise. My wife and I will cruise from the Mediterranean to Indonesia. I've never been to Bali; next year is the time to go there.

My firm is doing well. Over time I've brought into the company leaders who are smart and really know our products. They think much like I think. We have a good culture and a strong culture. I can truthfully say that the top three management levels (out of five) are all on board with our company and its culture. Life is good.

Sorry to say, now is the time to start worrying. Beware when all people speak well of you. Sounds like you are all so happy, things are going so well, you are tempted to coast along. All your top people think alike. They see the world the same way. It appears you are not worrying much about your competitors or about the new technologies that are coming along. What about the disruptive technology that the upstart company down in Texas is rolling out? What about the new regulations those crazy legislators and their minions in Congress are proposing? Who is thinking outside the box? What is challenging the status quo?

Who or what is cannibalizing your business? Are you so afraid of losing your existing customers to one of your own potential new services that you won't start the new service? Are you like the phone company that wouldn't start cell phone service because the firm might lose some landline customers? That phone company no longer exists.

You need to shake things up, and get out of the comfortable rut you and your folks are in. Start to think more about the future, five, ten, fifteen years from now.

Here's a good one. Set a goal next year of spending 25% of your time worrying! When you are dead you can stop worrying.

Board Membership: Take It Seriously

Are you a member of a board for some organization? Then take your responsibility seriously.

Here are some things to do. First, show up for all meetings, and make sure your name is on the list of attendees. Second, think through all proposals that come to the board and vote prudently, legally, and ethically. Make sure your vote is recorded by your name. Make sure there are minutes for each meeting and the minutes are approved in a manner congruent with company bylaws.[14]

Do not be a pass-through board member. A pass-through board is one that does whatever the CEO or the executive committee suggests. As a board member you share responsibility for board actions, so think through your votes and board activities and vote for the most beneficial directions of the firm, not just what the CEO recommends.

Protect yourself. Make sure your board is protected by directors' and officers' liability insurance. Your company and your board may be sued for almost any reason, and you need to be protected. The courts appear to be increasingly willing to penetrate the corporate shield and go after individual board members for improper decisions. Make sure there is an ethics committee and an independent audit committee to review the work of the board and head off improper decisions.

Be very familiar with your company's articles of incorporation. Make sure that all actions of the board are congruent with corporate requirements.

Don't rely solely on the corporate attorney. The corporate attorney's job is to protect the firm, and the interests of the firm may not be the same as your personal interests.

Be very careful about conflicts of interest. If you are involved in an activity that even has the appearance of putting you in a conflict of interest with the organization, make sure that the activity and your involvement in that activity are reviewed and approved by the board.

---

[14]Resource: White, B. J. (2014). Boards that excel: Candid insights and practical advice for directors. Berrett-Koehler Publishers.

If there is an issue to be voted on which involves a conflict of interest, be sure to recuse yourself and make sure the recusal is noted in the official minutes.

Keep copies of minutes of all board meetings held during the time of your membership. Keep those minutes for several years as advised by your attorney.

Board Culture

Boards have cultures. Typically the culture has developed over time, is based on past members, past decisions, and past ways of doing business. Members who have served for long periods are accustomed to the board's culture, and attempts to modify it radically are typically resisted. Newcomers soon learn the culture and may be able to modify it marginally. A group of newcomers may be able to make more significant changes.

The board structure and culture are often determined by the type of firm being governed. Not-for-profits will typically have a culture different from for-profit firms. In for-profit firms, the culture is typically different if it is a widely-held stock firm. Small firms headed by an entrepreneur will have a culture which is of another type.

In a small firm headed by an entrepreneur the board will typically exist to meet the legal requirements, but has little de facto work to do in managing the firm. The CEO is typically the board chair, and the board members may be family members or relatives, or members of the management team of the firm. The board meets once a year to satisfy legal requirements but takes little or no independent action.

Not-for-profits often have a self-perpetuating board whose members are dedicated to the mission of the firm. Alternatively, the board members may be appointed by supporting organizations, such as a college board whose members are appointed by the supporting denominations. The work of these boards is mainly to appoint the CEO, who then is the prime mover in actions that are brought to the board for approval. These boards are sometimes referred to as pass-through boards.

When one gets to larger for-profit corporations, particularly those with widely held stock, boards may become more independent of the firm management. These kinds of boards often view the board as an active governing group and work closely with the firm's management in developing new thrusts and determining the direction the firm is taking. With these kinds of boards conflict can develop between the board and management, and disagreements can go public and involve the shareholders in the controversies.

If the board is truly independent of management, an important feature of the board culture is the relationship between the board chair and the CEO of the firm. The interpersonal relationships between these two individuals partially determine the culture of the board. Based on this relationship, the board culture may be highly contentious or supportive of management.

Whenever there is an independent board, a good culture will be one that allows conflicting opinions to be expressed and considered. Board members should be encouraged to avoid groupthink. Good cultures will promote the concept that no one individual speaks for the board, unless authorized to do so. Good cultures will promote full documentation of meetings and recording of votes on a person-by-person basis. Good board work will require appropriate legal endorsement of actions taken. Boards must be protected by adequate insurance to shield board members from unwelcome legal action.

For most of U.S. history of corporations, individual board members have been protected from legal action by the corporate structure unless, of course, the board member conducts criminal activity. It appears now that the courts are more willing to penetrate the corporate shield and go after individual board members for actions taken in the governance of the firm.

Given the possibility of legal action downstream, board members should be sure to be present for all meetings and their attendance duly noted in corporate minutes. All actions taken by the board should be approved by vote in which the vote, yea or nay, of each member is recorded. Minutes must be prepared and approved in a manner established in the company's by-laws. The by-laws of the firm must be followed religiously.

One place where board members may easily get into trouble is in conflict of interest situations. Board members must be self-policing about this issue. If a board member is in a conflict of interest state with respect to the firm, then the board member should normally recuse him- or herself from action related to that matter. The minutes of the action taken should state that the member by name has been recused from the action.

Board members of most firms will have their expenses paid to attend meetings and do the assigned work. Board members of larger firms will often receive pay for their board membership.

If you are given opportunity to serve on the board of a company, take the work seriously and do the assigned work conscientiously. You may have much enjoyment making a contribution and seeing your firm blossom.

Embrace Science

Don't fight science.

It's been surprising to me over the years to discover that so many people distrust science. There come to mind beliefs such as:

The United States didn't really land a person on the moon. It was all a fake.

Climate warming is false.

Aliens built the Egyptian pyramids.

Carbon dating is a hoax.

Vitamin X can cure cancer.

Genetic engineering is evil.

Immunizations cause autism.

All sorts of conspiracy theories surround scientific topics, and many kinds of theories which are based in people's imaginations are promoted as fact and believed as science by a lot of people. Much of this thinking partly comes from misunderstanding what science does and how it works. Some of it comes from giving science *too* much credence.

My message is: be very careful if you distrust mainline science, and be especially careful of embracing ideas that have no basis in good science research.

What scientists are trying to do is to explain and predict phenomena. Science is strongest when it can do both, that is, explain the phenomena of interest in terms of accepted science, then predict the how, why, and when of future occurrences. The search is not for ultimate truth, truth with a capital T. Rather it is about theories that work. Remember the famous equation $E = mc^2$? Is that the ultimate Truth? Who knows? But one can use the theory surrounding this equation to explain how bombs work and it can be used to build real bombs that blow up.

Scientists try to develop models, or comprehensive theories, that take account of all known facts about the phenomenon in question. As time goes by and new facts emerge, the theory gets substantiated, modified, or thrown out.

Then new models emerge that incorporate the now extended body of information. Science is self-correcting as time goes by.

As one model is discarded and a new model emerges, the preponderance of scientists will gradually shift their thinking from the old way of looking at things to the new way. In that transition period it may be difficult for the layperson to know what the best science is, but scientific knowledge will be cleared up over time.

Some people don't accept scientific findings because they are afraid of new things. They are worried that some bad unknown will result from the new science or technology; some bad consequence will occur that no one foresaw. Being cautious they reject the new. An example that comes to mind from recent news is the idea of seeding the clouds to change the weather. Some people think that very bad things may happen because we try to change the weather. In this case, the technology and practice have been around for many years and have not caused the catastrophes that worry some people.

This type of thinking is also exemplified by people who reject genetically modified foods. Even though the FDA runs about 200 tests on a food before pronouncing it acceptable, that is not enough for some people to overcome their fears that something bad will happen 20 or 50 years from now because of eating that food.

A problem with this risk avoidance approach to life is that one can't prove a negative, so one can't ever be sure that something untoward may not happen downstream. My attitude is, work with all we know, think about the possible consequences that can be predicted, then move ahead.

Some people don't accept part of current science because they think it violates their religious beliefs. As a practicing Christian, I don't know of anything in modern science that contradicts my understanding of God and the Scriptures. I am not afraid of science. I think science continues to show the marvelous universe which God created and in which we are privileged to live.

My particular theological tradition is the Wesleyan-Methodist-Anglican-Catholic tradition of Christianity. One of my Christian heroes is John Wesley, an Anglican priest who was leader of the Methodist movement in 18th century England. Wesley embraced the science of his day and wasn't afraid to try new things. He embraced the pre-evolution theories of his day (25,000 levels of life). Wesley used electric shock therapy which has been in and out of vogue since Wesley's time. He accepted the science of spontaneous generation of life. He wrote a biology book for his followers. He communicated with Benjamin

Franklin about science topics. In other words, he was not afraid of the science of his day. He sets a good model for us.

Some argue that we should not fool with nature, and particularly should not fool with people. However, all of my acquaintances who argue this way will undergo invasive surgeries and take medicine to maintain their health and extend their lives. So why is some invasive work with the human body okay and not others?

My personal measure of acceptance of science is this: When 90% of the scientific community agrees on a scientific model, I'm willing to accept that model as my working model and I make decisions based on that model. In terms of religious beliefs, I think God wants us to use our brains, and those of scientists, to carry on His creative work as we live our lives and work for Him.

Company Culture: Another Management Tool

Companies have cultures. Managing the company culture is one of senior management's top opportunities and responsibilities.

Several definitions of culture have been proposed. Trompanaars wrote that "culture is the way a group of people solve problems and reconcile dilemmas." Barnouw wrote that culture is "a way of life of a group of people, the configuration of all the more or less stereotypic patterns of learned behavior, which are handed down from one generation to the next through the means of language and imitation." Adler described culture as: "something that is shared by all or almost all members of some social group, something that the older members of the group try to pass on to the younger members, and something (as in the case of morals, laws and customs) that shapes behavior or... structures one's perception of the world."[15]

Culture is an amalgam of legends, stories, rules, rituals, ways of thinking, initiations, physical facilities, orientation procedures, rewards, awards, penalties, handbooks, communication methods, jokes, symbols, greetings, training, and so on. Culture is "the way we do things around here."

Companies have cultures. Culture is not separate from the company—it is the company.

---

[15]Resource: Trompenaars, F. & Hampden-Turner, C. 1998). Riding the waves of culture: Understanding Diversity in Global Business (2nd ed.) New York, NY: McGraw-Hill.

A **strong** company culture is one in which there is a great deal of consistency between rhetoric and action. Companies with strong cultures are characterized by: good communication; good teamwork and cooperation; higher productivity; more focus on work getting done than on politics; clear tasks and responsibilities; high morale and motivation; and worker involvement in decision-making.

A company may have a strong culture, but if it is not aligned with the company's strategic direction, the culture may not be a good culture. A **good** culture is a strong culture aligned with the company's strategic plan.

Company executives can determine the company culture. It normally takes several years to turn a large company's culture around. It will take the determined interest of the senior executives to move the company in the direction of the strategic interests. But it can be done.

Company culture is a tool in management's tool-kit. The culture must be aligned with strategy, and the CEO must make sure they are aligned.

Take Advantage of Crises

A few years ago I was associated with a firm that was in the doldrums. We were getting along, barely. We were paying our bills; growth was very slow. Morale was problematic. Not much exciting was happening. The firm was too fat and needed to be slimmed down. Too many products were being offered that were not selling. But management didn't feel strong enough to bring about the significant changes that would be needed to put the firm on a growth path. The needed adjustments would require some changes in personnel and in leadership and dropping some product lines. The senior management didn't want to stir up trouble, so little was done.

In that atmosphere, one of the VPs told me that the firm needed a crisis to move it ahead. He thought it would take some kind of catastrophe to bring home to the firm and its management the message that the present course was going nowhere. Further, a crisis would provide the cover for a weak management to make the needed changes. So, let's hear it for a good crisis!

Well, that may be pushing it a bit. I'm not suggesting that one ought to go out and create a crisis. Senior management should be making the needed changes when the firm is well and not in a crisis. Senior leaders should do good strategic planning and move the firm in the targetted direction before calamity occurs. Immediate action is needed, not putting off unpleasant decisions and execution.

Sometimes a crisis will come along and it will be too big a crisis for the firm to recover. The firm may have to close or sell out to another firm. If that occurs, then the firm's closure or takeover by another firm may leave problems in the community; the goodwill the firm has built up over many years can be quickly lost. Many people may lose their jobs. The facilities may have to be sold at fire-sale prices. Stockholders will be hurt. Wouldn't it have been better for leaders to have made the changes before things got so bad? If they had, maybe some people would have been disadvantaged, but not the whole firm.

Take two lessons from these considerations. Leaders should handle problems when they occur, not let them fester for months and years. Take care of the problem, or the problem person, and move on with life. Second, get ahead of the strategic curve. Make the necessary changes while the firm is healthy, while there is some cushion; don't wait until a crisis limits the moves the company can make. But if a crisis does occur, take advantage of it.

Brands and Branding

Does your firm have a brand? Can you describe it, picture it?

A firm's brand is very important to the health of the firm. Brands have monetary value. Brands help position the firm and help it market its goods and services.

A brand has many parts, many aspects. It is partly a visible symbol, perhaps a sign that is used by the company. But it is much more. It is also the image that comes to mind when the symbol is seen or the name heard. It involves the reputation the company has with respect to its goods and services. It is related to the good will the firm enjoys.

One of the most valued brands is Coca Cola. One recent estimate was that the value of Coke's brand was over $79B.

Brands are important to small and large businesses. A small, one-property business should integrate its signs, logos, stationery, property appearance, and all visible representations of the firm. The property must be kept spotless, well-maintained, and functional. Service must be excellent so the firm can attract and retain customers and clients.

Multi-property companies have more challenges in branding. Here there must be discipline so that all units of the company have similar looks, similar goods and services, similar signs, logos and stationery. Service levels should be consistent across the system.

We see good examples of branding in strong franchises. Corporate headquarters will insist on similar looking properties, similar products, consistently good quality, and consistent HR practices. If one sees a MacDonald's sign, one will know in advance what products will be available and their quality level. Franchises that lose control of their franchise sites may soon see deterioration in looks, services, infrastructure, maintenance, cleanliness, and brand.

Brand is very important in not-for-profit enterprises as well, such as church denominations. Denominations with strong brands—Seventh-Day Adventist, Church of Jesus Christ of Latter Day Saints, the Salvation Army—each have properties which are recognizable by their appearance. Church services are similar from one location to the next. There is a canon of songs that is sung in worship services across all locations. The theology is the same from location to location. Just as with franchises, denominations that lose their connectional cultures may substantially weaken their brands as each site goes its own way.

Enterprise leaders need to choose and manage their company brands. Brands and branding must be a conscious tool of strategic management.

Organize For Growth

I have a couple of friends who run a successful service business. Business is good. They have so many customers that it takes six weeks to get in to see them for service. They are happy and are making money. I have talked to them several times, over a period of several years, about expanding their business. But they respond by saying they don't want to expand. They like things the way they are. Growth would bring some problems that they currently don't have to worry about.

In my experience I haven't run across many businesspersons like the two described above. Most of the businesspeople I have dealt with do want to grow. They want to serve more people, or they want to have more influence, or they want to make more money. The problem with many is, while they want to grow, they don't know how to do it.

Some won't grow because the leaders won't take risks. They are comfortable with their present operations and environment, and know that any significant growth would require borrowing money, or bringing in new staff, or implementing new ways of doing business. They just can't get up the courage to make the move.

Some won't grow because they don't know how. They know how to run their current level of business successfully, but don't understand how a jump in size would be managed. They aren't willing to bring in consultants to show them the way, or they are not willing to hire staff that can provide the leadership needed to get the uptick.

Some won't grow because their present organizational structure impedes growth. Their present structure has been worked out over a period of years and serves the present quantity and quality quite well. Growth cannot occur because the organization can't serve the increased numbers well. A growth spurt may occur, but the added customers degrade the firm's performance, customers leave, and the firm settles back to its previous level.

The burden of this message is to encourage leaders to organize now, in advance, for the next level of the business. If your business is currently serving 200 customers, organize for 250 and then increase your customer base. Continue increasing your service capability so that you can grow and retain your customers.

This approach of organizing for growth works in non-profits and well as in for-profit firms. Let's look at Protestant churches in the United States. The average church has about 100 people attending. There is typically one pastor. The pastor knows everyone in the church, knows the kids, visits the sick, marries the young, and buries the dead. People expect that level of service from the pastor. If there is some growth in attendance, the pastor won't know the people so well, won't be attending all the families' social functions, and can't make all the hospital calls. Some parishioners who were there when the church was more intimate will feel left out, and they may not be so welcoming to newcomers. So over time the church will settle back to its previous levels where everyone was comfortable with the all-responsible pastor.

It turns out to be difficult for a church to jump from 100 people attending to 250 attending. It's also difficult to go from 250 to 500, and so on. Members who used to be big fish in a little pond may become little fish in a big pond. The larger operation requires a different culture and a larger set of staff running the church functions.

The church pastor who wants to grow the church will have to sell the benefits of the larger operation and organization to the existing parishioners to get them to buy into a growth culture. The church will need to put personnel and structures in place which will make the church receptive to new congregants.

Seldom, whether one is talking about for-profit businesses or not-for-profits, does growth precede cultural and organizational change. Usually the change precedes the growth.

Mergers and Acquisitions: Strategic Tools

Two of the tools in your toolkit of strategies are Mergers and Acquisitions (M&A). Since it is difficult to determine from the public press reports whether a given action is a merger or an acquisition, for purposes of this note I will not distinguish between them. I'll refer to each as a merger.

Your firm A may want to acquire or merge with another firm B for one or more reasons. Perhaps firm B has intellectual property that you want to acquire. Perhaps B has a talent pool you could tap, or products that would complement your list of products. Maybe it has a geographic distribution you could add to your company. Maybe B has a pile of cash to acquire. Perhaps it has political connections which you could use. Maybe there are physical resources that could enhance the new joint structure. Maybe you can acquire B, keep some parts of it, and sell off the rest. Maybe your firm and B are in the same general line of business and you can consolidate operations, save money, and raise your profits.

In considering a merger there are many matters that should be considered. Of course, cost is very important. Another extremely important consideration is culture. Two cultures have to be brought together to create the culture of the newly merged firm. Research shows that one of the principal causes of failure of mergers is related to culture. One significant example of failure was the merger of Mercedes and Chrysler. This was billed as a merger, but many observers opined that it really was a takeover of Chrysler by Mercedes. The two cultures were so incompatible that the newly merged firm never did click, and eventually there was a break-up. Another example is the merger of Compaq and H-P. This HP-Compaq merger held together, but reports indicate there was a lot of wailing and gnashing of teeth. Now that merged HP has split into two corporations.

Another consideration is that the acquiring firm also takes on all the written and unwritten obligations of the acquired firm. Perhaps the success of the acquired company depends on tacit knowledge of its workers. Perhaps its success depends on relationships. Perhaps the acquired company has unwritten understandings with its stakeholders that are important to its business. The acquiring company gets all these environmental artifacts along with the formal structure.

Bringing two firms together requires much advance work. Care must be taken to see that all levels of the two firms are properly educated about the merger, its whys and wherefores. There is usually a great deal of fear, because some people may lose their jobs in the process. All the stakeholders have to be properly prepared. The post-merger work is also important to keep the merger on track and successful.

Sometimes leaders of poorly performing companies think that merging with or buying out another company will give them the boost needed to return to success. That may or may not work. If the acquired company also is doing poorly, then the merger of the two poorly performing firms is not likely to bring success. As the saying goes: If two dead people get married, they don't have kids.

So mergers can be successful, but the merger must be done carefully with much advanced planning. Keep M&As in your tool kit, and use them wisely.

Succession Planning

What happens to your company if the CEO drops dead? What happens if the Chairperson of the Board drops dead? What happens if your head scientist moves to another company? Who takes over if your head attorney has a heart attack in the middle of a trial?

These untoward events happen quite often, to the dismay of stakeholders. As a result stock values may drop. Key information may be lost and company thrusts seriously impaired. Decisions that need to be made immediately may be left undone. In a not-for-profit key donors may withhold funds. Political fights may emerge as people jockey for an unoccupied position. Emergency meetings of the board may be necessary with resulting disruption of board members' work and lives.

An often overlooked part of strategic planning is succession planning. Many times key leaders do not want to think about dying or getting ill, and they ignore the necessity of developing plans for continuity of the enterprise. It's too late to upbraid that leader for failure to prepare for the future if that leader is now dead.

It is the responsibility of the board to develop succession plans before some catastrophe happens. Policies and procedures must be in place to fill key vacancies within a few hours of the vacancy occurring.

At the least, interim officials should be appointed with appropriate responsibility and authority to carry on the work of the firm.

One aspect of succession planning is mentoring. Each key leader should be mentoring one or more individuals to prepare them for filling that leader's position. The individuals being mentored should have access to key information and plans so he or she can step in without losing much time and effort.

One *Fortune 500* firm had a policy that each key individual had to recommend three individuals who, in that key leader's estimation, could fill that leader's spot in the firm. The goal was that if a key leader dropped dead or was otherwise incapacitated, his or her position could be filled in 24 hours.

Of course, a firm should have policies that protect key individuals and their work. Health programs and memberships in athletic clubs are often used. Key leader insurance is a common practice. Policies regarding travel have the goal of keeping key leaders out of harm's way; policies that prohibit multiple key officials flying together are quite common as well. Nevertheless, while the firm may try to mitigate risk, accidents happen, and people die or leave, so the company must be prepared.

At a lower level in the organization another hedge can be undertaken, and that is to cross-train employees. If a lower level employee gets sick or leaves, the cross-trained employee can fill the gap on a temporary basis and keep the machinery rolling.

Who are you mentoring to take your job? Who are you cross-training to prepare for unfortunate events?[16]

Recruirment vs. Incruitment

Companies spend scads of money trying to get new customers, clients, or patients. New customers represent increased revenues and give the company opportunity to serve more people. A net increase in customers may improve the firm's market share, and that is good. So let's get the sales team out and about and ask them to bring us some new customers.

While recruitment is very important, some firms fail to look at one very important pool of customers, the ones the firm already has. The current customers have already made one decision to identify with the firm, so a first barrier has already been passed. Much research

---

[16]Resource: Maciariello, J.A. (2014). *A Year with Peter Drucker*. Harper.

shows that the second sale to an existing customer is easier than the first sale to a new customer. The lesson is that firms should pay significant attention to current custowers and make a significant effort to sell new goods and services to existing customers.

Various metrics have been used to study existing customers and their departure from the firm. The firm should know what its *retention rate* is from period to period, or to say it another way, what its *leakage rate* is. There should be studies of departing customers to determine why they left the firm. Was it customer service? Did the firm's products or services not meet the needs of the customers? Do the firm's goods or services not have the cachet, or the bells and whistles that customers want? All in all, firms should keep in close contact with their existing customer base to keep the customers as happy as possible.

If our firm is producing physical products, we should work to produce very high quality products. Maybe our firm should adopt and use a quality-inducing philosophy such as Six Sigma. Whatever method of quality control we use, we should be asking customers what they think about the quality of our products. Constantly remind customers that we value their input.

We should always have the goal of creating *customer delight*. Customer delight means going beyond the requirements of the contract with the customer. Doing the unexpected and striving to make the customer happy should be our object. So INCRUIT and RECRUIT!

Watch What You Say

Wise persons over the ages know that the tongue can get a person into lots of trouble. There are several Scriptures in the *Bible* that speak about the tongue, such as:

> Keep your mouth closed and you'll stay out of trouble. ~ Proverbs 21:23

> So also the tongue is a small thing, but what enormous damage it can do. A great forest can be set on fire by one tiny spark. And the tongue is a flame of fire. ~ James 3: 5-6 both from *The Living Bible*.[17]

People realize that speaking unwisely will often cause more difficulty than remaining silent. It's better to wish one had said something than to regret having said something that will come back to haunt you.

In centuries past our words could get us in trouble with another person, or we could write something that would take our thoughts to a

---

[17]Resource: *The Living Bible*. (1971). Wheaton, IL: Tyndale.

distant point given enough time. But now we can get in trouble, world-wide, in an instant. With the communication links we now have, our words can go to thousands of people almost instantaneously. Further, a word sent privately to one person can be forwarded to thousands of others.

Thoughts we intended only for close confidants may go viral, and our reputation and careers may be severely damaged.

We have heard many stories of people who sent something over social media which came back to haunt them. One story I heard was about a man who complained about the new boss. He thought he was sending the complaining e-mail to a friend, but he hit the wrong button and sent it to all the firm's employees. He was terminated within a week.

Kids who don't understand the consequences of sending confidential messages and pictures often get caught sending something deleterious to a friend. The friend then passes it on to his or her friends, and soon it is out there to folks for whom it was never intended.

Messages put out in social media are sometimes retrieved by potential employers, and many individuals don't get jobs because of postings they have made.

It's quite clear that employers have access to business networks and computers used by their employees at work. So don't write anything or post anything to any e-mail system that you wouldn't want your mother or an antagonistic lawyer to read.

Obeying the Boss

Should you obey the boss? If the boss says "Go," you go. If the boss says "Stay," you stay. That would be heaven for the boss. For most of us, however, the notion of "obeying" strikes a wrong note. We don't like to think we have to obey anyone; we are our own boss, we do what we want, when we want it, and the way we want it.

But of course, that doesn't work so well if you are working for someone else. You have to be amenable to the boss' requests, and carry them out in a reasonable timeframe and at a high quality level.

Perhaps we can learn something from the monks and members of religious orders who for centuries have lived under vows of obedience. The Rule of St. Benedict, which influenced most of the religious orders in Christianity, prescribed three vows for members: poverty, celibacy, and obedience. Lay versions of these vows would be: modesty, chastity, and obedience.

On first hearing it sounds like the monk is to be blindingly obedi-ent to his superior; whatever the superior wants the monk to do, the monk must do it. But that's not the way the philosophy of obedience has developed. Both the superior and the subservient monk must be obedient.

Because obedience is so important, it has been the subject of much study and discussion over the centuries. Over time religious scholars identified several levels of obedience. One extreme is represented by "I will do it if I have to, with wailing and gnashing of teeth." A better reaction would be "I will do it and try to have a good attitude." An even better reaction would be "I will do it and love doing it." While the sub-servient person has an obligation to obedience, the superior has an obligation to listen to the subservient person and treat the subservi-ent person with respect. Obedience is a two-way street; the boss and employee are obedient to each other, but in different ways.

Now let's leave the monastery and move over into business prac-tices. We first make the assumption that the boss and employee are thinking and moral persons. That being the case, the boss will not ask the employee to do anything immoral or unethical. If the boss did ask such, the employee has no obligation to carry out the boss' command. The employee does have the obligation to point out to the boss the immoral or unethical nature of the command, then be willing to suffer the consequences of being fired or forced to resign.

Now let's suppose the boss wants the employee to do something which the employee thinks is unwise. Let's suppose the action to be taken is moral and ethical, so there's no problem in those respects. But the employee may think the action will hurt the business and hurt the brand. Then by the philosophy of obedience, the employee has the duty to bring his or her concerns to the boss and explain to the boss why the proposed action will be harmful. Once the employee has made her concerns known to the boss, then the employee's obligation has been met. If the boss still wants to move ahead with the desired action, the employee should then go ahead with the required action. It would be hoped the employee could take the action with good heart and do his best to make the action work to the good of the firm. If so, the employee has met her obligation to obedience.

Guard Your Passwords

Protect your passwords. Start at the beginning with the passwords you choose for your various accounts. Don't pick your name, your birthday, your mother's name, your address, your city, your car, your dog, or anything that would point a thief to you. Pick a random combination of letters, numbers, and symbols. Don't use the same password for multiple accounts. Don't store your passwords in your desk or under your computer keyboard. Find a secure place to keep the passwords. Don't let your family members know your passwords, and don't let them use your passwords. Keep them secret from everyone. Not your girlfriend or boyfriend either.

On the other hand, if you were to become incapacitated or die, your spouse or your attorney should know where the passwords may be retrieved. If you keep a list in your safety deposit box, only your box co-signees or your executor will have access.

If you have an expert in to work on your computer, you should stay with the expert while he or she works on your computer, and you should enter passwords as needed during the work. Don't let the expert see your passwords.

Double your access control. Where possible set up your accounts so that both passwords and key question responses are needed before access can be made.

Be careful of password consolidators. These are spots on the internet or in the cloud where you can list and retrieve your passwords. Make sure any consolidator you use is itself accessed only by a very secure process.

Watch for scams. You may get an e-mail claiming to be from some company which calls for you to provide your e-mail password. Don't give it!

Keep Your Appointment Times

It is most frustrating to have an appointment at a doctor's, dentists, or lawyer's office and then be kept waiting for the appointment to begin. You are paying good money to the professional, and your time is worth a lot, but you have to keep waiting because the professional can't manage his or her appointment calendar.

Also, one of the most frustrating incidents for any manager is to be kept waiting for a scheduled appointment in the work setting. The manager may have worked hard to be on time for the appointment, but then is kept twiddling her thumbs while the person to be visited goes on and on with a previous appointment. The waiting person is wasting expensive time. When the appointment does get started, there is already a frustration level that must be cooked off to have a productive meeting.

It is especially frustrating when the person holding up the appointment is the boss. The waiting employee can't complain too loudly about the failed meeting time or the boss may get mad. These unthinking bosses cause dozens of hours of productive time to be lost each day if the failed schedule culture is rampant in the firm.

Just as you are frustrated about being kept waiting, you should make sure that people meeting with you are not kept waiting. You should work with your secretary to allow plenty of time for appointments, then religiously keep to the schedule.

There are many tricks you can use to keep yourself on schedule. One is to notify the person you are meeting with what the agenda will be and the decisions that need to be made. Another is to build in a buffer time of a few minutes between appointments. Still another is to ask your secretary to notify you five minutes before the meeting is scheduled to end. Also, you can always have the meeting in the other person's office, then you can leave at your own initiative. Finally, if it appears you really do need extra time, then schedule a second meeting. In summary, you need to be religious about keeping to your appointment schedule and establish an office culture of being on time.

Customer Information

Do you drive your customer nuts by asking for the same information over and over again? For example, when your customer comes or calls for a service, must he or she go through the whole litany of questions about that customer's company or the customer's personal information? If you have two buyers from the same company, does each one have to supply the company information whenever he or she asks for service?

In this day of integrated databases, it is irritating to customers to have to supply the same information over and over again. It is time-consuming for both customer and supplier. It may mean that the supplier has multiple databases with the customer's information stored in several systems.

DON'T DO THAT. Get the customer to supply the information once and only once. Make it easy for the customer to purchase your goods. Whenever a company rep has a contact with a customer, put a report on the contact in the one data base. Typically ask one question about base information: Is the information we have on you up to date? If not, just get the updated information; don't start all over again.

I had an experience recently that irritated me greatly, this one dealing with a medical procedure. Involved were the doctor, the doctor's company, and the facility where the procedure was performed. I gave my personal information to the doctor's company, including my insurance information. I had to sign a release form for the procedure. The company representative said my information would be sent to the facility that performed the procedure. The day before the procedure was to be performed I got a call from the facility with a long list of questions, many of which had already been answered. Then we got to the day of the procedure. I went in and got a long list of questions, many repeating the questions of the day before. Further, there was a bunch of releases to sign. There were five at the desk. Then I went in the procedure area of the facility and had to answer more questions and fill out two more release forms. Some of the questions were the same as the ones I had answered not a half hour before. Then finally the doctor came to perform the procedure, and there was another release form to sign. Altogether there were eight release forms I signed, some of them duplicates of others. The procedure itself took about 20 minutes and was done well. No complaints with the medical procedure itself.

As the opposite extreme, I was reminded of hotel companies which collect your reservation and information in advance. When you get to the hotel you walk in and go directly to your room. The hotel has sent all the information including door entry to your phone. You don't have to give the information over and over again.

Here's another tip. Don't ask for information you aren't going to use. Don't ask for information you might use sometime in the distant future. Don't let the company attorneys talk you into collecting all sorts of information that is of interest only in esoteric situations. Why does the company need to know your paternal grandmother's maiden name if your security access information has already been established? Why does a company need to know where you lived before your last two moves? Why does a company need to know your religion? Now one may be able to think of a reason why each of the questions above or similar others might be needed; if so, the company should be prepared to offer an explanation why the information is needed and how it will be used.

Summary. Ask your customers for the data once and only once. Ask only for the information you are going to use.

Wasted Time in Meetings

Every day in the United States hundreds of thousands of valuable hours are wasted in meetings. These meetings may be one-on-one, or may involve 5-15 people, or may involve dozens. Lots of them are un-organized, or management fluff, or off-topic, or dominated by a few people, or too much time spent on an irrelevant topic. Many people attending these meetings will be thinking about other things, worrying that their real work is not getting done, and leave frustrated. It's worse when the wasted meeting is conducted by the boss; it's hard to kick against the pricks.

If planned right and led right, meetings can be valuable management tools. But it takes thinking, work, and discipline to make them constructive and effective. People contemplating meetings might consider the following tips.

First, decide if the meeting is really needed. If the goal is just to share information, it might be better to send out the information in electronic form. Second, just because a group has a regular schedule of meetings, don't go ahead with a meeting unless there is specific action that needs to be considered.

If it is determined that a meeting needs to held, then plan it carefully. Set up the agenda and give the agenda to the participants in advance. (I had a boss once that refused to go to a meeting unless he was given an agenda in advance). Send out all handouts in advance and ask everyone to study the handouts before the meeting. Make sure that each agenda item has a presentation leader who is appointed in advance. The agenda should list the topics of all decisions that are to be made during the meeting.

The overall leader of the meeting should estimate the time that is to be spent on each item and make sure the scheduled time limits are observed. The overall leader must assure that the discussion sticks to the topic at hand and not go off on irrelevant tangents. If it appears that one topic is going to take too much time, then adjust the schedule or move the topic to another meeting, or appoint one or more persons to make a decision about that topic.

A good book to read for additional tips is Blanchard and Johnson's book *The One Minute Manager*.[18] One specific tip from the book is the Stand-Up Meeting. In the Stand-Up Meeting the participants don't sit down. They deal with the topic or topics quickly, make the appropriate decisions, and leave.

Finally, be rigorous about starting and stopping times for your meetings. Get started exactly on the announced starting time. Don't wait for late comers. Stop on or before the scheduled ending time. Don't cause the attendees to be late for their next duties.

Don't Burn Your Bridges

Epworth had worked for the Sigmoid Corporation for 15 years. He was a middle-manager responsible for operations in the Southern California area. Back at the corporate office in Indianapolis the Senior VP for Operations retired, and corporate was looking for a successor. Epworth applied and thought he had a good chance of being appointed.

Unfortunately for Epworth, corporate went a different direction and brought in an outsider for the VP position. That disappointed Epworth and made him mad. He flipped out, wrote some excoriating letters to the CEO and complained at length to colleagues in his local facility. He really raised a stink.

A month later the CEO was visiting the California facility and called Epworth to a meeting. At that meeting the CEO gave Epworth the axe and told Epworth his services would no longer be needed. The reason the CEO gave was the fit Epworth had about the promotion. Epworth's actions and attitude had degraded his value to the firm. Epworth had burnt his bridges, much to his sorrow.

Another story. Eileen (not her real name) was an important assistant in a retail firm. Eventually things went sour and she decided to leave the firm. Before leaving she changed the passwords in many accounts and took off, leaving the office high and dry. Then she asked for a recommendation!

The message from these stories is: Don't burn your bridges when something untoward happens. Don't get mad and take your frustration out on the firm. Keep your cool and move ahead with life.

You can't predict what will happen downstream because of decisions made. If you get the promotion, don't lord it over others because

---

[18]Resource: Blanchard & Johnson, (2003), *The One Minute Manager*, William Morrow.

one of them may be your super at some point in the future. If you don't get the promotion, the person who was promoted over you may at some point report to you. Maybe you didn't get the promotion you wanted because senior management has something else in mind for you.

When you leave your firm, don't badmouth it. Don't tell everybody off and write nasty letters to the boss, colleagues, or the newspapers. Don't spread rumors. These kinds of actions may work to your disadvantage more than cause problems for the firm. Also, you will want references, so keep as good relations as possible. If the firm makes a decision you don't like, hold your peace. Don't burn your bridges behind you.

Little Things Mean a Lot

Little things can turn off your customers. Little practices your company has may send a subtle message that you are eager to serve customers, or that you are not ready to serve them. Here are eight practices that companies need to make routine.

Business Hours

Make sure your business hours and days are published. Put them on the doors of your business and put them on your website. Customers need to know when they can do business with your firm. Then hold to those hours faithfully.

Unlock Your Doors

Make sure all external and appropriate internal doors are unlocked during your business hours. If you have a door that is not unlocked for some security reason, be sure to put a sign on the door telling the customers where they can conduct their business.

Turn on the Lights

Make sure the lights in your business are on during business hours. The outside lights and all inside lights should be on. Make sure the lights in the bathrooms are on or will automatically turn on when a person enters a bathroom. Don't ever leave a customer or employee in the dark.

Safety Signs

Post signs and mark floors to improve safety. Just because you and your employees know about hazards, don't take it for granted that customers also know where danger may lie.

Waiting Areas

If your business is such that a customer may have to wait a while to get service, make sure the waiting area is welcoming. Have comfortable chairs. Have up-to-date reading materials. Have free coffee available.

Have Personnel on Site Who Can Take Care of Business

Don't have all the principals go on vacation at the same time. If the business has one owner and one assistant, make sure one is available at all times. Train the assistant to take care of as much business as possible.

Have Receptionists who Smile

Have you gone to a business where the receptionist keeps a dead face when he/she greets you? Or worse yet, a sourpuss? Train your receptionists to smile when a customer comes in. Make sure the receptionists act like they want to help the customer, not make the customer feel he or she is interrupting the receptionists' work.

Train People Who Answer the Phone

Make sure your phone answering people answer with a smile. When they first pick up, make sure they identify the company and themselves and inquire how the caller can be helped.

Company Communication

With the advent of the Internet and many social communication channels, expectations about communication in a firm have altered remarkably. Practices that were in vogue fifty years ago are now passé and, in fact, quite troublesome to the modern firm.

Let's explore some of these changes by first looking at the communication practices of several decades ago. The main characteristic of communications inside the firm was that they were hierarchical. A firm of any size would have a wiring diagram which represented the reporting lines in the firm. Any person on the chart was supposed to communicate to the person directly above or directly below her. Jumping over the person above was considered as "going over his head" and was a no-no. If Susan had an idea about some activity in the company, she had to report it to her immediate supervisor who, if he liked it, would pass it on to his superior, and so on until it got to someone who had authority to act.

If Susan wanted to contact someone in another division, she was supposed to run the information up the ladder until it got to a person who was at the administrative level of and connected to a comparable person in the other division, who in turn would receive the communication and pass it down to the target person. Of course, this often took considerable time.

Decision-making was much more hierarchical as well. A person who was authorized to make a decision didn't necessarily think it wise to share his thinking with his subordinates. He was the one who had the information, so he should make the decision, implement it and let life go on.

Now let's look at the current situation. First, we have numerous communication channels, as mentioned above. Second, information is now much more readily available. There are multiple sources of information about the firm available to every employee. Firms make much information available. There are publicly available reports that go to many government entities. Third, employees expect and are expected to know much more about the firm, its vision, mission, products, and services. Employees are often asked their opinion about directions the firm should take for its future. In short, company cultures have changed considerably in the last 50 years, I would argue, for the better.

Given this new culture, who talks to whom? These days there are still wiring diagrams that lay out the hierarchy. These diagrams are usually less deep than they typically were decades ago. And inhabitants of the firm still talk to people above and below them in the chart. But the restriction on talking to others several levels above has considerably relaxed. Now we expect that information should be given to the person who needs to know it without having to go through several intermediaries.

So how is the hierarchy protected so that company chaos doesn't result? One way is to look at the wiring diagram again and make two copies of it. In one version there are lines all over the place. This version of the diagram is the communication diagram. The second version is the more traditional version. This is the decision-tree version. Substantive decisions go up and down the hierarchy.

So what does this all mean to Bill Smith, who is a middle level leader in his firm? First, he can talk and communicate with anybody in the firm. Most of his communications will be with his supervisor, immediate colleagues, and subordinates. But he doesn't try to use the communication channels to get decisions made that are above his pay-grade. For these decisions he moves up the hierarchy to his immediate supervisor, who in turn takes it further up as necessary. To further assure that communications don't step on toes, he always copies in his boss when communicating with other people in the firm who are outside his close circle of colleagues.

These old and new ways of communicating sometimes come into conflict between older and younger people in the firm. The older people may even try to impose a gag rule on communications. Little they realize that the world has changed, and gag rules seldom work.

Watch Out For Bogus Stats

I like numbers. All my adult life I've worked with numbers as a sometime Professor of Business and Mathematics. I have taught numerous statistics courses at the undergraduate level and quantitative methods at the MBA level. Statistics is a powerful tool that can lead to all sorts of good results that can be used in business management.

Well, sometimes I don't like numbers. Numbers can get you into trouble. Numbers can be massaged, manipulated, multiplied, divided, and made to say all sorts of things that are not justified by the raw data. Buying into numbers without due diligence can get you into all sorts of trouble and lead to bad business and personal decisions.

We are constantly bombarded by propaganda items that attempt to use numbers to prove some point. Many times the numbers don't prove anything at all. A recent example was a poll that was taken over the Internet. The pollster was trying to show that Democrats are different from Republicans in certain ways. The pollster developed some questions, put them out on the net, and asked people to write in with their opinions. An impressive 114,000 people responded. From the results the pollster derived a complex theory about the difference between the two political parties.

Unfortunately, the pollster's report didn't support the conclusions. There was no attempt to get a representative sample of the population. The pollster didn't report the questions that were asked. The pollster didn't give level of significance information. Altogether it was a report of a study that lacked credibility. I suppose the pollster thought we would be impressed because 114,000 people responded to the questions. Bad use of statistics.

Areas where there are lots of problems are health products, medical treatments, and foods. Someone will come up with a new vitamin package and ask 30 people to try it. Twenty-nine come back and say they feel better now that they are using the new product. That report is used in marketing. It sounds good, but it is not good statistics and doesn't prove much.

Recently there has been a spate of advertisements for prostate problems. All sorts of medicines are advertised that can fix the problems. Some of these claims are unproven and the advertisements are unapproved by the Food and Drug Administration.

We often hear of wonderful procedures used in other countries to counter serious diseases, such as cancer or diabetes. A doctor comes on the screen and says that 40 people came to his clinic in country X, were treated by this new therapy, and 38 of them were cured of the problem. The problem is we don't know the credibility of the people, we don't know if they are fudging the data, and it was not a controlled experiment. Bad use of statistics.

The social sciences like to use correlation statistics to show relationships between two sets of data. It's one thing to show a significant correlation between two sets of numbers; it's another thing to show any causal relationship between the two phenomena from which the data come. This happens so often that the social sciences might be labeled as the correlation sciences.

Watch your graphs. Graphs can be arranged to make the data being graphed look big or small. Small changes can be made to look big, and vice versa. Be sure to label the axes of your graphs and show where the data originated. Don't leave the interpretation to the viewer's imagination.

Use statistics with care. Make sure the people who are generating the statistical reports know their statistics theories. Make sure that when a statistical theorem is used that all the criteria for using the theorem are satisfied. If not, the result may sound good but be nonsense.

I have been fascinated over the years by the book titled *How to Lie with Statistics* (Huff, 1954, Norton)[19]. This book contains lots of exam-

---

[19]Resource: Huff, D. (1954). *How to lie with statistics*. New York, NY: Norton.

ples of bad uses of statistics. The examples are old, but the principles are current.

So be skeptical when reading statistical data. Remember the saying attributed to Mark Twain: "There are liars, damn liars, and statisticians."

Gender Relationships

Many leaders get into trouble because of problematic gender relations they have with other persons in their firm. Careers have been derailed because the leader did not use good sense in the way he or she conducted amorous relationships. Marriages have been wrecked because of gender problems at work. But by following a few good rules leaders can avoid a majority of these problems.

Here are a few rules that give direction to gender relationships. First rule: Never date anyone who reports to you or over whom you have power. These relationships can turn sour very quickly and can result in charges of sexual harassment.

Second rule: Don't allow yourself to get into compromising situations with a person of the opposite gender. A perfectly innocent situation can go south if you don't protect yourself.

Here are some things you can do to protect yourself. First, put a glass door on your office so the meetings you have are not hidden. This may protect you from being accused of some hanky-panky in your office. Second, be careful when you go out to meals with a person of the opposite gender. Make sure your assistant knows about the meeting, that it is noted in your scheduler, and the purpose of the meeting is recorded. Be sure to tell your spouse or significant other about the meeting. Third, be super careful about trips out of town with a person of the opposite gender. Make sure you have separate rooms. Keep track of your activities, and check in with your office regularly.

Third rule: Don't discriminate by gender in hiring or promotion decisions. Unless your firm is under a court order to hire or promote in a particular way, always hire or promote the person best fit for the position as based on the job description and/or the bona fide occupational qualifications.

Fourth rule: Make sure there is no compensation discrimination based on gender.

Fifth rule: Be careful in conversations. Don't tell off-color jokes. Don't comment on other persons' attire.

Sixth rule: Don't be touchy-feely. Only touch a person of the opposite gender by shaking hands (in U.S. culture). Don't hug, kiss, or embrace.

Following these rules will reduce the risks of getting into an unethical or immoral situation, and they may protect your career.

Wrong Metric

It is important to use metrics in management decision making. But it is not just a question of using metrics, but also one of using the right metrics.

I am intimately acquainted with a firm that has a clash of metrics. The players are: Sales, Production, and Senior Management. A senior metric in the firm is AMOUNT OF REVENUES.

In this firm the sales people are working hard to get new customers. The metric for this unit is NUMBER OF CUSTOMERS. This number is going up, so the sales folks are getting pats on the head for good work. The PR department puts out the message that the company is growing.

However, the production people are making and providing product to those customers, and the average sale per customer is going down. In fact, total sales are going down. In other words, in terms of the senior metric, AMOUNT OF REVENUES, the picture is not so good. In fact, the number of production workers has been reduced. Production folks are unhappy with the sales folks because the sales folks are not bringing in heavy buyers.

Now in many companies there is a cultural clash between sales and production; the clash is almost expected, it happens so often. Sometimes the sales people sell and commit to too much product and the production folks can't keep up. The situation is different in the firm described above. In the firm described above the sales folks are bringing in the wrong kinds of customers.

Another poor use of metrics is to manage on the aggregates or averages. Averages can hide both good and bad activities. Consider this simple example. One year Division X had net losses. Division X was considered by senior management to be a dog, and it was proposed to sell off Division X. However, Division X was a collection of five units, three of which were profitable and two which were not. Further, the three profitable divisions met the revenue targets and burden expectations of the firm. These three were doing very well.

By looking beyond the aggregate, senior leaders chose to keep the three profitable units while selling one unprofitable unit and closing the other one. In other words, senior management escaped a bullet by managing on the details rather than on the aggregate.

Conglomerate Chiefs: What Value Do You Add?

Jonathan Westfield is the Chairman and CEO of the Windfall Corporation. Windfall is the holding company of a conglomerate of eight subsidiary corporations with non-overlapping products. Each of the corporations has a board and a CEO. Windfall's corporate expenses constitute about 1% of the combined revenues of the eight subsidiaries.

Windfall has a small staff, with Westfield as the principal. For each of the eight subsidiaries Windfall has a liaison officer. Windfall has a VP for finance and a VP for HR who interact with the VPs for Finance and HR of the eight subsidiaries.

Windfall's board is pleased with the progress the eight firms are making with respect to revenue, growth, and profits. They are beginning to question, however, the value of having an umbrella holding company. They are starting to discuss what value the umbrella corporation is adding to the eight firms. Each of the firms seems to be doing well. What can Westfield point to that Windfall has done to improve revenues and profits of the eight firms? Why have a conglomerate if the umbrella firm is not adding value?

These types of questions need to be considered by leaders of conglomerates. What value does the umbrella corporation bring to the total package of corporations the umbrella controls? If the senior corporation is not adding value, why keep the conglomerate? Bust it up and let each subsidiary go its separate way.

Of course, there are activities the senior corporation can do to increase the value of the complex. The officers of the senior corporation can help set the strategic directions of the individual firms. The senior officers can be mentors to the CEOs of the individual firms. The senior firm can set performance targets for the firms and can assist in succession planning. The senior firm can assist in raising financing, and the senior firm can carry on lobbying activities on behalf of the conglomerate. Senior officers should check on each of these activities and see if they are producing tangible results for the corporation. If not, maybe a bust-up is in order.

One trap officers of the senior corporation may fall into is to micromanage the subsidiary companies. Normally each firm should run on its own power with minimal oversight from the senior corporation. Interaction between each firm and the senior corporation should be restricted to big picture, long-term strategies and their execution. If the senior corporation has to interact too much with one of its firms, then perhaps that firm should get new leadership so it can move forward on its own.

Of course, if one of the firms comes into hard times, the senior officers may step in and assist in bringing the firm back to health, or may decide to spin it off. But that type of involvement should be exceptional, not the norm.

Back to Westfield and Windfall. Westfield proposed to the board that it undertake a six months study of the value of maintaining the conglomerate. After the study is concluded, it is hoped the questions raised above, and others, will be answered and a decision made about Windfall's future.

Risk Management

Life is about taking risks. Running a business is about taking risks. As a business leader you will face many kinds of risks. The trick is recognizing the risks and mitigating those risks as much as is prudent.

Some risks, if they are realized, lead to catastrophic results. They may have very low probability of occurring, but if they do, catastrophe and chaos may result. For example, if your country gets into a nuclear war, you, your family, and your business may disappear from the face of the earth. When you consider the mitigating options available to you, you may decide there is nothing reasonable that can be done and you'll just live with the risk.

Other types of risks may be mitigated more easily. For example, if your company has any possibility of being flooded out, you buy flood insurance. You have fire insurance to cover your company in case of fire. Liability insurance and officer's insurance cover other types of risks. Getting a good insurance broker will help you identify the various kinds of risks your company may face and will help you acquire the coverage you need.

Here are a few more risks you should consider and mitigate. What happens if your CEO drops dead or is killed in a plane crash? Do you have insurance coverage for this eventuality? Do you have succession plans in place so the company can move ahead without loss of momentum?

Do you have plans in place for physical and personnel security? What happens if a gunman or a terrorist team invades your property? How are you providing protection for your people and property? Do your employees and security people know what to do in such an eventuality?

How are you protecting your data? Suppose you have been proactive and established the best system security you can, but nevertheless your computer system is hacked into and information about your customers is stolen? How do you react? Do you have backup for your financials as well as your customer and product information? How are you protecting your intellectual property?

Suppose you lose your main production facility to fire, tornado, or a bomb? Where and how soon can you begin production again?

One company in our section of the country is very concerned about someone gaining computer access to its production facilities. To mitigate against this risk, the company has cut all but one computer tie from its facility to the internet. All thumb drive ports on computers are disabled. Because the company has one high technology component made by another firm, that outside firm is allowed to run tests on that single component for 15 seconds once a quarter. That single tie is the only outside link with the company's production facilities.

Physical security is becoming more and more important as terrorism and disgruntled shooters get more notoriety. Limiting access to facilities, and even limiting employee access to certain sections of the facilities is becoming more and more common. There are now several large international firms that provide physical security to plants around the world.

These examples show just a few of the risks companies take. Your job as leader is to identify as many risks as possible, analyze their probability of occurring and the fallout that would occur if the bad event happens, then take prudent steps to mitigate the risks.

Motivating Employees in the United States and Elsewhere

Studies show that many employees in U.S. companies are not fully engaged with their work. Due to this lack of engagement their productivity and morale suffer. Many scholars have tried to analyze what motivates employees and, given that information, how to motivate the employees to tighter engagement with the firm.

One such scholar was Abraham Maslow, who developed a five-level hierarchy of needs. The base level is Biological and Physiological Needs. Next higher is Safety Needs. Then Belongingness and Love Needs. The fourth level is Esteem Needs. The fifth and highest level is Self-Actualization. This is a hierarchy of needs, and in general the lower levels must be satisfied before the higher levels can be met. Maslow argued that leaders, in attempting to motivate their employees, should use this hierarchy wherever possible, moving each employee up the hierarchy. The theory is that employees who are situated at the higher levels will be better motivated and engaged.

Later in his career, Maslow added a sixth level, which some call the Spiritual Need level. This level supersedes even the Self Actualization level.

Much research shows that this hierarchy of needs is quite useful in the United States and other countries which have low context cultures and are characterized by individualism. However, the applicability of Maslow's hierarchy for motivation does not work so well in cultures which are high context and group oriented.

A hierarchy which was developed for a high context culture is the *I Ching*, a philosophy developed in China two millennia ago. The I Ching philosophy has nine levels of need. The lower levels correspond somewhat to Maslow's lower levels, but the higher I Ching levels focus more on the good of the group, rather than the good of the individual.

Much research has been done on a culture by culture basis as to what motivates employees. Leaders who are working outside the United States should avail themselves of the research and use the applicable research to motivate the employees under their leadership.

Cash Flow

You can be wealthy and broke. It all depends on the cash you hold.

The leaders of Hamilton Massey (HM) were in a good mood. As HM came to the end of the last quarter of the fiscal year the firm's stats showed that the number of customers had increased by 20% over last year's final quarter. The firm's PR department put out a Christmas letter which bragged about the increasing influence HM was having in its industry.

However, all was not rosy inside HM. In fact, things were downright bad. HM did not have enough cash to pay some of its key suppliers, and had to go hat-in-hand to those suppliers and ask for a one-time extension. HM got the one-time extension from most of its suppliers, but had to agree to financial penalties.

Investigation of the firm's financial practices revealed that the firm's salespersons were beating competitors' prices by granting discounts on sale prices. With those reduced prices HM's salespersons signed up a bunch of new customers. But word soon got around and similar discounts had to be extended to continuing customers. The totality of the discounts meant that HM was not bringing in enough cash to pay its bills, let alone securing a profit for the firm.

Management knew that salespersons had authority to grant discounts, but it was assumed the discounts would be minimal. Management failed by not giving good guidance to the sales force. Further, leaders had been paying attention to the balance sheet, which showed good numbers. Because the financials from the first three quarters of the fiscal year looked good, the leaders did not pay sufficient attention to the last quarter's stats as the quarter developed. They especially didn't pay much attention to the cash flow sheet, much to their later dismay. The CFO was dismissed and the CEO did not get her normal bonus. It took three years for HM to recover.[20]

This short story gives us some important lessons. First, a firm can get in trouble fast. Leaders must pay continuous attention to the numbers and background policies. Second, leaders must pay attention to cash flow. The firm must have enough cash to meet its payroll and pay its bills. Failure to keep up with its obligations can lead to poor morale, can cause the firm to lose key personnel, and can significantly damage the firm's reputation. Stock values may plummet and the firm may get into a death spiral that leads to bankruptcy. Third, a firm can have a strong balance sheet and still have a cash flow problem. In other words, the firm can be rich and broke. The firm's balance sheet may carry it for a while, but soon the lack of cash will dominate the firm which may need to convert assets into cash at fire-sale prices in order to get enough money to pay its obligations.

If a firm is in financial trouble and brings in a turn-around management expert to try to save the firm, one of the first things the new expert will probably do is to get hold of the firm's cash flow. In this situation it's not uncommon to cut expenses drastically to stop the outflow of cash. Once the cash drain is significantly slowed down the

---

[20]Resource. Reuvid, J. (2015). *The business guide to credit management: Advice and solution for cash-flow control, financial risk, and debt management* (2nd Ed). Kogan Page. [First edition is 2010].

expert can then turn to other management decisions that need to be made to save the firm.

The message to be put next to the CEO's and CFO's hearts is: Manage your cash flow.

Budgets

What is a budget? There are about as many definitions and uses of budgets as there are managers of budgets. It's all over the place.

Actually, budgets, budgeting, and using budgets are all wrapped up with a company's culture, its DNA. Most of the time it's historic in the company: That's the way we do things around here. The same processes and execution go on year after year without much scrutiny.

Budgets may be used in different ways in the same company. Some units are provided both an income budget and an expense budget. These units are expected to bring in so much money and spend so much money. Other units are expense centers, with no income expected. Managers work their expense budgets with instructions not to spend more in each category than is given on the budget sheet.

In terms of execution, budget managers have a tendency to spend all their expense budget allocations. They may argue that if they don't spend their expense budget allocations, then next year's expense budget allocations will be cut.

Budget managers who have responsibility only for the expense side of life, or have responsibility for both revenues and expenses without a profit target, will often reduce budget expenditures until the end of the fiscal year. Then toward the end of the fiscal year when they see how much money is left they will go on a buying spree and spend out their expense allocations.

I was associated with a firm which each year had a company-wide spending spree toward the end of the fiscal year. The CFO got wise to what was happening, and about a month before the end of the fiscal year put a freeze on expenditures. The next year the spending spree occurred slightly more than one month before the end of the fiscal year. So the CFO moved the freeze up another month. The game between the CFO and budget managers didn't work, so business soon went back to that firm's normal.

In terms of setting budgets, the easiest method is to do incremental budgeting. That is, choose some percentage and raise all expense budgets by that percentage. That makes everybody happy and mad. Units that need additional money don't get it, and units that need to be reduced don't get reduced. This is the *business as usual* approach which leads to mediocrity.

Some firms build expense budgets as zero-based budgets. Every unit has to predict and justify what the expenses will be for the next budget cycle. That information is brought together by central leaders and decisions are made as to which predictions are valid, then allocations are made. This is a good approach, but is very time consuming.

Unit managers will often pad their budgets. That is, they will underpredict their income and overpredict their expenses. Then when the fiscal year ends and the revenue is better than predicted and the expenses are lower than predicted, the manager looks very good. Senior leaders have to be wise to budget padding.

Some companies put budgets in concrete and never allow variation from the numbers. Managers know to not ask for exceptions, and know they must bring in the revenue target. Only the most drastic change in the environment would cause the senior leadership to modify the budget: nuclear war, government collapse, and, oh yes, bankruptcy.

Ideally, a budget should be a numeric representation of the strategic plan. That is, the strategic plan, which covers many budget periods, should lead to tactics which cover the next budget period. The budget is then set to move the company forward on its path to realize the goals of its strategic plan.

Budgeting for strategy calls for a strong central leadership. Leaders must make the hard choices that will move the firm in the right direction. In this approach expense authorizations will move around. Some units will get higher authorizations and others lower. New units may be started. Some units may be phased out. Central leaders who don't like controversy will not like this approach, as some units will see themselves as getting gored and will blame the leaders.

Ideally, budgets should not be put in concrete, but in a semi-solid state. We live in a dynamic economy, with new competition coming online, with new technologies constantly emerging, and with legal environments changing. As a result, tactics and maybe even strategies get modified. There should be mechanisms to allow changes in the budgets as the firm moves through the fiscal year. It may not be prudent to wait for the next budget cycle to make modifications.

Another good practice is, wherever feasible, make budget managers responsible for both sides of the budget and build in incentives for profits. That is, set targets for revenues, expenses, and net profits. If the budget manager beats the targets for net profits while keeping all the rules, that unit gets a benefit of some sort for its good work.

One last point. The budget can be used as one of the tools to assess whether the firm is executing on its strategic plan. Since the budget is a representation of the plan, failure to keep company activities congruent with the budget may mean the firm is not executing its strategic plan.

In closing, let's go back to the main point above. Budgets should be a reflection of a firm's strategy. Go to the trouble of building a strategy-based budget; it will pay off over the long haul.

Allocating General Income, Expense, and Overhead

Allocating general income and overhead to the various budget units in a firm is mostly an art, and a little bit of science. An untoward allocation of either income or expenses can lead to bad decisions about product sustainability and can lead to loss of morale in units that appear to be mistreated.

Let's take a look at both sides of the ledger, first the general income. Firms have multiple income streams, some of which are attributable to a specific product. For product-induced revenue streams, the totality of those streams should be allocated to that product and its budget unit. One might think of this as direct product income, and allocation is easy.

Not so easy is general income that doesn't derive from a particular product. This may include interest income, general government appropriations, income from endowments, tax allocations, and gifts. It is more problematic to determine where to allocate these revenue streams across budget units.

One of the easiest, and worst ways of assigning overhead is to allocate on the averages. Suppose there are 10 income producing units and three expense units (including central administration), for a total of 13 units. The average approach would be to divide the total non-product income by 13 and attribute the average to each of the 13 units.

There are several other ways to slice the non-product income, including: by product revenue, by unit direct expense, and by decision of central administration in support of strategic thrusts. However it is done, if personnel surmise that their unit is not getting its fair share of non-specific revenue, much griping and loss of morale may result.

With respect to expenses, similar considerations pertain. First, find all direct costs associated with a product and assign those expenses to the product. Personnel, equipment, marketing, insurance, space rental, utilities, depreciation are all items that can be determined and the costs attributed to the appropriate product on an activity based accounting process.

Non-direct expenses, including overhead, can be allocated on the average as well. That is easy, but certainly not recommended. It is better to divide general overhead into categories and assign the overhead to the units that are serviced by that category.

For example, central administration personnel costs can be divided among the various product lines or budget units. It is relatively easy to determine for each administrator how much time that administrator works with each of the units under his/her purview. Then divide that administrator's compensation by the time spent on each area and assign that part of the compensation to that budget unit. Sometimes costs are allocated based on number of employees, square footage, or proportionate revenues.

Do not assign overhead from unit B to unit A if A does not use the services of unit B. For example, if the plant in California in the conglomerate has no interaction of any kind with the plant in Bosnia, none of the overhead from the Bosnia plant should be assigned to the California plant. As another example, if the R&D center in Brazil works totally on R&D for unit A, then none of the overhead from R&D is assigned to other budget units.

Be careful with full product accounting. Suppose a unit shows positive net revenue X when all direct income and expenses are taken into account. If general overhead Y assigned to that unit is greater than X, then X-Y will be negative and it will look like that that budget unit is losing money and the unit should be cut. What is not taken into account with this thinking is that X is being used to meet some of the general overhead expenses. If the unit is cut, its revenues and expenses go away, and X will not be available for meeting general overhead expenses. Other units then will need to take up the slack, making them look less profitable. Also, if the firm reports that the unit is running positive in terms of direct revenues and expenses, but at a loss because X-Y is negative, the firm would not necessarily be better off to cut the unit. Cutting the unit may make the firm worse off.

Customer Delight

QUESTION FOR STRATEGY BUILDERS. Can you turn normal, good customer service into customer delight?

Have you heard of *customer delight*? Customer delight occurs when the service or product supplier goes beyond high quality service, and does things for the customer that really pleases the customer and makes that customer an unofficial salesperson for the supplier.

Customer delight (and customer put-off) can occur in large and small companies. Here are some examples from my life, two from small firms and one from a large firm. I have no financial investments in any of these three companies.

Mexican Restaurant

I love Mexican food. My favorite Mexican restaurant in my county is located near my work. It is one restaurant in a small chain in Idaho. The family that owns the chain came from southwest of Mexico City.

This restaurant delights me. First, I like the flavor set of the food from the section of Mexico. I get that flavor set regularly and consistently at my local restaurant. Prices are good and comparable to the competition. The restaurant is clean and service is quick. So far so good, but dozens of restaurants could claim the same. What makes the difference and gives me delight? It is the manager. She knows her customers by name. She talks with me when I go in. She asks about happenings in my life. She is always upbeat. She is a hard worker. She has given me a couple of shirts that advertise her restaurant. Her influence on the wait-staff is apparent. The wait-staff also know my name and allow me to put in special orders that are not on the menu. The eating experience is a delight. I like to go there for lunch or dinner.

Car Service

The firm that works on my car is a company in downtown Boise that works on BMWs and two other foreign models. About 13 years ago I decided I wanted to get a BMW. I had wanted one for many years but didn't get one until then. I found a good BWM which was then 10 years old. It was in very good shape and was a good price.

The BMW had two previous owners. Those owners had all their service work done at the Boise car service firm, so the firm had all the repair records on the car. When I was considering buying the car, I took it to the same firm and asked the guys to check out the car and let me know if the car was in good shape. The guys and their crew spent four hours going over the car in detail and told me the things that would need repair or service and how much it would cost. They charged me $50 for four hours of work. I asked why they would charge me so little for the work they did. The answer was that they hoped to get my business and they would make up the money in later business from me. I was pleased with their honesty and direct answer.

I did go ahead and buy the car, and have had it serviced by the same firm ever since. Their costs are reasonable and I get personalized and honest service. They know me by name. When repair work is done they give me a complete explanation of what the situation is. Several times they have directed me to inexpensive solutions to repair problems, solutions I would not have known about. It is somewhat inconvenient for me to drive from Nampa to Boise to get service, but it is worth it to me. I am delighted. At the time of this writing I have 388,000 miles on the car. I love to drive it in the Idaho mountains.

Not So Good

Recently I had a prescription filled at a pharmacy in a local big-box company. I paid for the prescription and took it home. Unfortunately, I did not look at the bottle before leaving the store. I later discovered the pharmacy had given me the wrong prescription, at a significant cost. When the pharmacy was notified of the mistake, they said it was tough, there was nothing they could do because I had taken the medicine out of the store. So I was stuck with the wrong medicine and high cost.

Up to that point the pharmacy had given normal service. Costs were okay, and the prescriptions were completed in a reasonable amount of time. Now I have added that pharmacy to my Suspect List. When I go back, I am very careful to make sure that the medicine is what the doctor prescribed. I'll probably tell a few friends about the problem. Even though I still shop in the store, it no longer delights me.

Handling Moral Failures of Key Leaders

Have you handled a case of one of your key leaders being accused of illegal, unethical, or immoral conduct? What did you do in that situation? How did you handle the legal, personal, and business aspects of the case? How did you protect your firm, yourself, and the person being accused?

Many examples come to mind. There was a situation in which a key leader was arrested for solicitation of a prostitute. Another occurrence was an official who was caught by the janitor having sex with a subordinate in his company office. There was an example of a male employee watching with his binoculars the women in the housing unit next door and being accused of voyeurism. Another example was a senior leader who got drunk and made a public spectacle of himself by walking down a main street in the capital shouting as he walked along. Then there was the case of a male leader making off-color remarks to a subordinate. Another example was the vice president who embezzled a couple hundred thousand dollars. Still another was a senior leader who took a female subordinate up into the mountains for a "counseling session" which turned into something more; the subordinate filed a complaint the next day.

As you can see, these examples vary in terms of their seriousness and the culprit's relationship to the law. If the matter is a felony, your ability to work with the situation may be limited because it may be taken out of your hands and treated by the law officials; you as leader just follow along as the matter gets adjudicated. Your main job may be to try to control the public relations fallout from the incident.

In some companies there are Class A rules which, if broken, leave no choice in how the matter is handled. Some companies have a no-offense policy about sexual abuse; the guilty party is dismissed with no second chance given. If the offense you are dealing with comes under a Class A rule, then you will have to execute the penalty based on the rule.

There may be other situations that are not so serious in terms of violation of the law or violation of a Class A rule. Then you may have some freedom to assess the violation and determine the consequences for the parties involved.

One principle to be used is to protect the reputation of the firm as much as possible. If the violation was public with a public scandal, then your course of action may be quite different from what it would be if the violation was private. If the violation is publicly known, you may need to have a public airing of the situation and make the penalties known to the public. Further, your options in working with the culprit may be limited. You may have to dismiss the culprit to restore morale inside your firm and restore the firm's reputation.

If the violation is private, you may have more options in working with the violator. If the violator is otherwise a good and productive leader, you may want to try to save her or him and keep the person with the firm. You may be able to set up counseling, and/or establish a means of restitution, to try to assure that the injurious behavior does not happen again and the violator develops new and correct behaviors.

There is another aspect to these considerations. Suppose a person is accused of skullduggery but denies that it happened. It may be a matter of he said-he said, or he-said she-said, with no collaborating evidence available. How do you treat this situation? We know that a career can be ruined by a false accusation, so you as leader must do what you can to protect your people from the fallout of false accusations.

If the accusation against one of your employees is coming from outside your firm, you may want to involve your firm's lawyers in protecting your employee. Your lawyers will do whatever they can to keep confidences and to shield your firm as much as possible from untoward publicity. Your lawyers will recommend to you courses of action which you can activate to protect your firm and your employee as appropriate.

If the accusation comes from within the company, your HR policies and the HR office will probably be involved in working with the situation. If there is an accusation of immoral or illegal conduct brought by an employee, that employee should be required to put the complaint in writing and given to the appropriate officer in HR. Then, following company policy, the matter can be investigated without the accuser's identity being made known to the accused, at least at the beginning of the investigation. At some point, of course, the accused may have the right to confront the accuser, again, depending on company policy and the law.

After appropriate investigation by the HR office, the disposition of the matter may be recommended to you for your final decision and action.

One last matter. By law you will need to protect the privacy of most individuals involved in these kinds of actions. While the person impacted may be able to tell all sorts of stories about you and your disposition of the matter, you will not be able to divulge relevant information. Be prepared to be criticized by other individuals who only know part of the story.

As you can see from this brief discussion, these matters can become complicated very quickly. You will need all the wisdom you have, and the advice of your lawyers and HR officials, to handle these types of problems without undue damage to your firm, to the culprit, to the victim(s), and to yourself. Whatever you decide to do in handling the untoward situation, you need to consider all those involved. If someone has been violated in any way, you won't want to add to his or her grief.

Chapter 4

Odd Thoughts

U. S. Manufacturing: A Story of Success

When I was in college about 25% of the U.S. workforce was engaged in manufacturing. About 4% were involved in agriculture, and the rest were in various kinds of services. At the time of this writing only about 11% of the U.S. workforce is involved in manufacturing. Rather than being a downer, this is a miracle story of success.

The United States is producing more physical goods than it ever has in its history. But it is doing it with a far lower percentage of the workforce than in the last 100 years. The reason this can happen is that worker productivity has gone up spectacularly. Aided by automation, robots, and artificial intelligence, each worker on the average can produce two or three times what the average worker could produce 50 years ago.[21]

There is a misconception in the common wisdom that the United States is losing out in the manufacturing sector. Many believe that manufacturing jobs are going out of the United States and the United States is losing ground. Indeed, many jobs have left the United States, but those are largely jobs that are labor intensive and don't require much sophistication. These routine jobs get offshored to China, Viet Nam, the Dominican Republic, or a dozen other countries. However, the offshoring of these kinds of jobs is slowing. In fact, many of those jobs are starting to return to the United States.

There are several reasons for jobs returning to the States. One reason is that wages are rising in many countries, so the savings formerly obtained from cheap labor are reduced. Added to that, costs of tariffs, transportation, and insurance eat up more of the profits. The Buy U.S.

---

[21]Resource: Hagerty, J. (2014). Decimated U.S. Industry Pulls Up Its Socks. *Wall Street Journal*, December 26, p. B6.

campaign is also influencing some companies to return work to the States.

However, when the work comes back to the States, many of the jobs won't return, for when it comes back it will be done with less people using sophisticated machines that don't require as much labor.

A couple of years ago I visited a stocking company in Istanbul, Turkey. The company turns out hundreds of different kinds of beautiful sockwear. The socks are sold largely in the European Union and northern Africa. In visiting the production floor I found 300 sewing machines, each requiring one worker to sew socks. An inspector roamed the floor sampling the output of the machines to check on quality. The company is doing quite well; in fact, it is planning to expand and add a couple hundred more machines.

I was highly impressed with the company, its output, and its management. But then a second thought occurred. That way of making stockings is already out of date. All those sewing machines and people can be replaced by machinery driven by computers that can make high quality stockings faster and cheaper. Given that the people will no longer be needed, the stockings don't have to be made in a developing country where labor is cheaper than in the United States. The modernized stocking company can locate in any country and can contribute to that country's manufacturing output, but not much to its labor count.

What we have seen in the last 50 years is a major restructuring of the U.S. economy. Now only about 2% of the workforce is in agriculture and 11% is in manufacturing. As more and more work is brought back to the United States, U.S. manufacturing production will go up, but labor counts will not grow much. It is my prediction that the percentage of the U.S. workforce engaged in manufacturing will never exceed 15%.[22]

Artificial Intelligence

Artificial Intelligence (AI) is an active field of research for psychologists and computer scientists. Millions of dollars are being spent each year in the attempt to get machines to imitate human thinking and communication.[23]

---

[22]Nutting, R. (2016). Opinion: US manufacturing dead? Output has doubled in three decades. Retrieved from http://www.marketwatch.com, 3/28/2016.

[23]Resources: Marcus, G. (2014). Artificial Intelligence Isn't a Threat—Yet. *Wall Street Journal*, Sat/Sun December 13-14, 2014, p. C3.

A basic problem, still unresolved, is to understand what thinking and intelligence really are. There are more questions than answers. Consider these questions: What is intelligence? Is there more than one kind of intelligence? What would a machine have to do in order to demonstrate that it thinks? Can a machine that interacts with only one intellectual domain be considered a thinking machine? What does it mean *to understand*? *to learn?* Do animals think?

Alan Turing proposed an operational definition of thinking. He asked that a computer be placed in one room and a human in another. The human isn't told what is in the other room, another human or a computer. The human and the computer carry on a conversation. If the human can't tell whether the responder (the computer) in the other room is a computer or a human, then we will say the computer thinks.

Some people ascribe intelligence to computer programs that play games. IBM developed Big Blue, a computer program that plays chess at world championship levels. IBM also developed Watson, an AI engine that can respond to natural language and provide information upon inquiry. In 2011 it was tested on the TV game *Jeopardy* and beat the human contestants it played against.

A *New York Times* article (10.13.14) reported that IBM was setting up Watson as a separate business unit, was investing $1B in it, and was developing a workforce of 2000 people for the Watson unit. At this writing about 100 companies are using the Watson engine.[24]

With the advent of massive storage devices and much faster speeds, information from millions of books and other sources can be stored and retrieved quickly and at will, so computer programs that provide factual information are increasingly common. Programs that hear and store spoken natural language and programs that speak in natural voice are being perfected. Significant progress is being made on computer programs that translate from one natural language to another. Speech and pattern recognition and machine vision are now gaining traction. However, there is still much work to be done on programs that tie together disparate facts or draw conclusions from complex arguments.

A report from Gothenburg University gives us insight into other developments in AI:

---

[24]Miller, C.C. (2014). Rise of Robot Work Force Stokes Human Fears. *New York Times*, Tues December 16, 2014, ppA1-A3

...a research team from Gothenburg, Sweden, has now been able to create an AI programme that can learn how to solve problems in many different areas. The programme is designed to imitate certain aspects of children's cognitive development.

In *artificial general intelligence* (AGI), which is a new field within AI, scientists try to create computer programmes with a generalised type of intelligence, enabling them to solve problems in vastly different areas.

http://www.sciencedaily.com/releases/2014/09/140923085937.htm

Many programs that use binary logic are used in decision-making applications. These use *If A, then B* type logic. Once it is determined that A has occurred, then the program will assert that B must occur.[25]

More complex are programs that use rules of thumb and probabilistic logics. A central feature of these AI programs would be something like: If A, then B 60%, C 30%, and D 10% of the time. One can see applications of this in medical screening. The computer would ask the patient a series of questions about symptoms of an illness or condition. The rules of thumb would be applied and a list of potential outcomes developed. From this list another series of *If, then* statements would be generated, and the patient would provide more responses. Given time and enough questions/answers, the program would eventually conclude with one or more potential conditions or illnesses. Then options for treatment can be explored using the same AI engines.

It appears that AI will have massive impact and be a disruptive technology to many in business and industry. AI is just now starting to gain traction, so get ready for a ride, maybe a bumpy ride, into the future.

Should Churches Be Run Like Franchises?

Robert Anderson was a serious young man who was interested in religion and spiritual matters. He was a member of a Reformed tradition evangelical denomination, the Geneva Evangelical Church. Late in his high school years Anderson went to the presiding bishop for the Southern California area and told the bishop that he felt called to the parish ministry. The bishop commended him on his intention and told Anderson to go to college and major in theology, which was what Anderson did.

---

[25]Movie: 2014. *The Imitation Game.* Story of Alan Turning and his work with the Nazi ENIGMA machine.

When Anderson graduated from college with his theology major, he went back to the bishop and presented himself for assignment. The bishop told Anderson that the Geneva Evangelical Church had no church in Jones Valley, a small city of 5000 population not too far from the Mexican border. The bishop said the denomination would pay his salary for two years if Anderson started a church in Jones Valley; after that Anderson's salary would have to come from the congregation he established. The church would not need to give any support for denominational activities until it was well established financially.

Anderson was excited and began his work in Jones Valley. He rented a hall and started Bible studies and services. He needed to put a name on his hall, so he called it the Jones Valley Community Church. The hall was a 50-year-old building that had formerly been used by the International Order of Odd Fellows (IOOF). All Anderson did was change the name on the front of the hall. Anderson decided that he would use contemporary music in his worship services, so he found a few musicians who would play in the church band and started singing choruses during worship services. He couldn't afford to buy Geneva Evangelical Church hymnals, and there was no established canon of choruses, so choruses varied from worship service to worship service. Anderson also served as church treasurer, collecting all the money that came in and depositing it in his personal account at the bank. He paid bills related to church work out of that account. Each Sunday Anderson preached a sermon. He read much evangelical literature, much of it from megachurches in the Southwest. This literature strongly influenced his thinking, so soon his sermons began to incorporate elements of theology that were foreign to Geneva Evangelical Church doctrine. After two years his congregation was numbering about 75 people for Sunday services. The congregants in Anderson's church did not identify with the Geneva Evangelical Church denomination. Anderson put in 60-70 hour weeks for the first two years of his ministry in Jones Valley.

For all practical purposes, Anderson's church in Jones Valley was an independent church. Doctrines being taught were not Geneva doctrines. The congregants were not aware of Geneva Evangelical Church's national and international programs. However, the bishop was very happy with the weekly attendance reports, and otherwise paid little attention to what Geneva Evangelical Church was doing in Jones Valley. He visited with Anderson for an hour once each six months.

Now contrast this with the typical franchise system based in the United States. Mary Johnson wanted to be a franchise owner for a national Chinese restaurant chain. She applied to the corporate office to start a franchise in her own city, population 40,000. As a first step she was vetted in depth by the franchisor. She had to show that she had the training, the skills, and the passion to become a franchise operator. She had recently graduated from college with a business major and a psychology minor, so she met the formal education requirements. She was also able to find the $200,000 start-up costs to purchase a franchise. The city where she wanted to start the franchise was also vetted by corporate.

After being approved and signing the contract, she was given six months training in running a franchise. Three months of that time were spent as a management intern in an existing franchise.

Getting ready to set up the franchise in her local city, the franchisor gave guidance on where the franchise property would be placed. The building was constructed to specifications established by the franchisor so the local property would carry all the visible features of the chain.

The products (the food), sold at the local franchise property were the products authorized by the franchisor. Prices were set by corporate. Human resource practices were dictated by the corporate office. Advertising was done using the accepted franchisor logo. Hours of operation were similar to those of the entire franchise chain. Local franchise budgeting was done according to franchisor standards. Care was taken to make sure that Johnson's personal finances were kept separate from the franchise's finances. Regular reports on many aspects of the local business went regularly to the corporate office. Corporate representatives came around monthly to make sure the local franchise was working at the standard and quality level dictated by corporate. The local franchise paid a fee to corporate for the privilege of using the franchise name, logo, publicity, products, and advice. Johnson found herself working 80-hour weeks for the first two years of managing the franchise.

The contract between corporate and the local franchise provided for a claw back of the local franchise if Johnson was not working out or the local franchise was not working to specifications.

Any Lessons Here? There are at least six lessons denominations can learn from franchise operations.

First, ministers must be trained and vetted before being appointed to lead a local church. They must be grounded doctrinally in the denomination's tradition. Second, they must be trained to run a business, for the local church is, among other things, a business.

Third, the denomination must give considerable attention to what is going on at the local church level. The presiding officer must be assured that the local minister is teaching and preaching accepted doctrine, not adding to or subtracting from approved doctrines of the church.

Fourth, the local church must be named with the denominational brand. Brand is very important to all types of businesses, churches included.

Fifth, the property should be kept up to high denominational standards. It should be kept painted, repaired, clean and functional.

Sixth, the church should be run with good business practices. Accounting for church funds must be done in detail. Spending should be transparent to congregants. Taxes must be paid. Withholding for employees must be sent to the government as required by law. The leader's personal finances must be kept separate from the church's finances.

Yes, many denominations could be advantaged if they adopted some practices from successful business franchises.

Chapter 5

The Challenge of the Future

Futurism

Futurism is a discipline found in some United States universities. In some universities it is possible to work off a bachelor's, master's, or doctoral degree in futurism. In the United States the discipline is called futurism; in the UK it is called futuristics.

Futurism as a formal area of study was born in WWII. As the name suggests, it studies what the future will be like a few years from now. There is the short-term future, 0-5 years from now; the medium term future, 5-15 years from now; the long-term future, 15-30 years out; the very long-term future, 30-100 years from now; and the ultra-long-term future: 100-1000 years out. One serious futurism book tries to project what life will be like 1000 years from now.

One of the tasks of the futurist is to describe alternative futures. If certain decisions are made now, what will that lead to in some named year in the future? Working backwards, given a particular desirable future, what must we do now to raise the probability that the desired future will be realized?

Futurism is not magic. It is well grounded in the traditional academic disciplines. Many of its practitioners are scientists and sociologists. Some are demographers who predict the human make-up of society in the future. Many government offices use long-term projections about the size and nature of the population as they prepare policies for government services. For example, many people in the United States have heard the discussions about Social Security and whether or not it will go broke in 30 years.

Futurists are found in think tanks, the military, universities, religious institutions, and government. Most of the *Fortune 500* companies have futurists on their staffs. They may be called futurists, or strategists, or long-range planners. For each company there is a need to project what society will be like and what the company should do now to prepare to sell its goods and services in the projected society.

One good source of ideas about the future comes from science fiction. Science fiction writers often can project ahead dozens of years with ideas that may come to fruition. Think of Jules Verne's books: *Twenty Thousand Leagues Under the Sea,* or *From Earth to the Moon.*

The principal organization in the United States that deals with futurism is the World Future Society (WFS). It is based in Bethesda, Maryland. The WFS has about 30,000 members. It holds an annual meeting each summer which a few thousand people attend. I have been a member of the society for about 30 years and over the years have taught courses in futurism. A few of my papers have been published in *The Futurist* or *Futures Research Quarterly. The Futurist* is a popular level magazine with articles from many disciplines. Most of its articles can be understood by college graduates. The web site for the WFS is: www.wfs.org.

Individuals can be futurists with respect to their personal lives. Think what you would like to be doing 10 years from now. What should you do now and in the next few years to make that desired future come to reality?

Future of Health Care

Health care in developing countries is changing rapidly. Billions of dollars are annually going into research about health care technologies and medicines. Health care philosophies are moving toward holistic medical care, integrated data bases in hospital systems, and inclusion of alternative medical practices.

Four significant developments for health care are the aging population, more operations by machines, home diagnosis, and shortage of health care personnel.

Aging Population

Populations are aging in developed countries. We can predict there will be increasing incidence of old-age medical problems, such as those related to heart, cancer, diabetes, and various mental conditions. Since a high proportion of expenditures for health care are spent during the last five years of a person's life, health care expenditures will continue to rise.

Operations by Machines

According to an article in the *New York Times,* over 75% of all prostate operations in the United States are done by robotics. This is suggestive of the trend to use machines for complex operations. Using robots, the lead surgeon in an operation will not need to be in the same room, hospital, or even in the country, to head up the surgery. A physicist reported that the electronic signals could travel back and forth fast enough from India to allow a surgeon in India to operate on a person in the United States. A surgeon in India could guide the machines through long-distance surgery.

Home Diagnosis

Another development will be software and home lab kits which will allow a person to do diagnosis of many health problems at home. Present practice is that a person has to go to a doctor and report all the symptoms to the doctor who then may check the symptoms on a software package to arrive at a diagnosis. The doctor may send the patient to a lab to donate some blood for a blood analysis or to get other tests.[26]

In the future there will be many apps for your communication device that will allow you to monitor your body functions. Signals will be sent automatically to medical providers for their review. You will be able to take pictures of your body parts and send them off to a medical professional for analysis.

Further, in the future there will be sophisticated software packages, based on artificial intelligence programming, which will allow you to enter symptoms. Further, there will be home lab kits tied to the software which will let you give a small amount of blood or other contributions and the kit will do the diagnosis and enter the findings into the software and, if necessary, send it on to a professional for a more complete diagnosis.

In addition to diagnosis, the software will report on a treatment regime. If over-the-counter pills or medical equipment are available, you may be able to self treat. Otherwise, you may still have to go see a doctor, or in some states, a pharmacist, or a physician's assistant, or the quick-care in a local big-box store, to get the appropriate drugs. Or perhaps you may order the pills by mail from another country. Of

---

[26]Resource: Topol, E. J. (2015). Your Smartphone Will See You Now. *Wall Street Journal*, January 10-11. pp. C1-2.

course, the diagnosis may require advanced treatments and/or surgery that would be provided by a medical expert.

Shortage of Medical Workers

The shortage of medical workers will continue into the foreseeable future. In many developed countries there is already a shortage of health care personnel; this shortage will exacerbate, at least in the near-term future.

Question: If these developments come to pass, how will that impact your business?

Embrace Change

One of my early mentors was Dr. Paul Schwada. He was a professor at the college I attended, an expert in educational philosophy (PhD from Illinois). Later he was a colleague of mine in another university. One of the main lessons I learned from him was captured in the phrase *Embrace Change.*

Schwada was a living model of the slogan *Embrace Change.* He was always a student of ideas and loved to talk about philosophies and theories and world perspectives. In his occupation as a professor he was always looking at new ways of doing things. He did not fight the new things that came down the pike; he embraced science and new perspectives on life and living.

I have partially embraced Schwada's philosophy. Part of my life has been characterized by change, but also some by constancy. For example, my commitment to Christianity has been a constant factor in my life. Although my perspective on the faith has modified considerably over time, my root belief and faith have been a foundation on which my life is built.

Another area of constancy is my marriage. I have been blessed to be married to Lois, the love of my life. She is a friend and a constant supporter. She is also part of the foundation of my life.

In other areas of life I have set routines which I follow day after day and year after year. As an example, for 30 years I have risen early each day and gone to work. I get there before anybody else in my building and get a lot of work done before anybody else shows up. Then the rest of the day I am not under the pressure that some of my colleagues exhibit.

My faith commitment, my marriage, and habits of the type described have provided a foundation, a stable base for my life. This stability has given me the freedom to embrace change in other areas of my life.

I would not consider myself a techie by any means, but I do like the communication technologies and the new products that constantly roll out. I see the positive benefits they provide and the way they can improve society, so I embrace the changes technology brings.

I'm also embracing the society which is developing here in the United States. I grew up when Jim Crow laws were prevalent, particularly in the South. Now we are trying, at least legally, to provide equality before the law and committing to treat all people with justice. In my view our country is much more advantaged to have among us people of many colors, religions and cultures. We are enriched by the diversity.

I'm also embracing new ways of doing my work. As a professor I have taught for many years in face-to-face situations. Now I have opportunity to work online with students. To me the online approach has been so much more rewarding because I can communicate directly with individual students in ways I could not before.

I note that many acquaintances are in changing job situations. Some are working for companies that have been bought out by another company. Some are in a buying company. Others are in job situations where the company has turned on its nose and moved in another direction. These changes may cause much anxiety because of an unknown future. Many of these same acquaintances embrace the change, dig in to the new environment, and come out as winners. Others get discouraged, fight the changes, and may not continue in their job situations.

Finally, I am embracing changes in myself. As I get older my body, my reactions, my senses are changing. I'm accepting those changes with good grace, I think. I'm not trying to fight them off and return to some previous age. Now is the best time of my life.

So let's keep our foundations firm, and then embrace change.

Which Upcoming Technologies Will Be Used?

There follows a list of technologies that have been introduced or may be introduced in the near future. Some will come into general use in their industries, and some will come into general personal use. We will say a technology is in general personal use in a country if 25% or more of the adults of that country use the technology at least once a week.

Select the top ten (or less) technologies which you think will come into general use or general personal use in the United States by the year 2025.

Once you have selected these technologies, describe how their use will impact your personal life and your firm's work. Also, describe how the selected technologies will be commercialized.

Here are some of the new and upcoming technologies:

Androids

Bionic Eyes

Bracelet Computers

Brain Transplants

Camera Drones

Computer Glasses

Designer Medicines

Driverless Cars

Embedded Computers in Brains

Embedded ID/Location Chips in Humans

Face Scanning Recognition

Fat Pills

Flying Cars

Force Fields

GM Designer Foods

Holograms

Invisibility Technologies

Medical Analysis Toilets

Microdrones

Mind Reading

Nanotechnologies

Personal Jet Pack

Photovoltaic Glass

Robotic Exoskeleton

Robotic Surgery

Satellite Based Electricity

Self-Cleaning Fabrics

Self-Heating/Cooling Clothing

Supersonic Commercial Flying

Thought-Control Prosthetics

3D Printing

2025
Your Personal Future

Look ahead a few years. Start thinking about your personal future.

1. How old will you be in 2025?   _   _   _   _   _

2. How old will your spouse be in 2025?   _   _   _   _   _

3. How old will your children be in 2025? ___, ___, ___, ___, ___, ___, ___

4. Where will you be living in 2025? _____

5. What will you be doing in 2025? _____

6. What one thing can you do now to improve the quality of your life in 2025?   _____

7. How much time and money are you willing to commit now to raise the probability that your desired life in 2025 will come to pass? _____
_____

Resources

Asimov, I. (2004*). I, Robot.* Spectra Publishers.

Blanchard & Johnson, (2003). *The One Minute Manager.* William Morrow.

Goldratt, E. (1990). *Theory of Constraints.* Great Bennington, MA: North River Press.

Hagerty, J. (2014). Decimated U.S. Industry Pulls Up Its Socks. *Wall Street Journal*, December 26, p. B6.

Hitt, M. A., Ireland, R., & Hoskisson, R. E. (2012). *Strategic Management: Competitiveness and Globalization: Concepts and Cases* (10th Ed.). Independence, KY: Cengage Learning.

Huff, D. (1954). *How to lie with statistics.* New York, NY: Norton.

Hurley, K., & Shumway, P. (2015). *Real women, real leaders: Surviving and succeeding in the business world.* New York, NY: Wiley.

Kim, W.C. & Mauborgne, R. (2015). *Blue Ocean Strategy: How to Create Uncontested Market Space and Make the Competition Irrelevant.* Boston, MA: *Harvard Business Review* Press.

Koch, R. (2011). *Strategy: How to Create, Pursue, and Deliver a Winning Strategy* (4th Ed.). New York, NY: Prentice-Hall.

Lawler, E.E, & Worley, C.G. (2006). *Built to Change: How to Achieve Sustained Organizational Effectiveness.* San Francisco, CA: Jossey-Bass.

Marcus, G. (2014). Artificial Intelligence Isn't a Threat—Yet. *Wall Street Journal,* Sat/Sun December 13-14, p. C3.

Maxwell, J. (2011). *The 5 Levels of Leadership.* New York, NY: Center Street

Miller, C.C. (2014). Rise of Robot Work Force Stokes Human Fears. *New York Times*, Tues December 16, pp A1-A3

Mintzberg, H., Ahlstrand, B., & Lampel, J. (1998). *Strategy Safari.* Prentice Hall Europe.

Movie. 2014. *The Imitation Game.* Story of Alan Turning and his work with the Nazi ENIGMA machine.

Pasmore, B. (2015). *Leading Continuous Change: Navigating Churn in the Real World.* Oakland, CA: Berrett-Koehler.

Porter, M. E. (2008). The five competitive forces that shape strategy. *Harvard Business Review,* January 2008.

Reuvid, J. (2015). *The business guide to credit management: Advice and solution for cash-flow control, financial risk, and debt management* (2nd Ed). Kogan Page. [First edition is 2010].

Techt, U. (2015). *Goldratt and the Theory of Constraints: The Quantum Leap in Management.* Dusseldorf, Germany: ibedem Press

Topol, E. J. (2015). Your Smartphone Will See You Now. *Wall Street Journal,* January 10-11. pp. C1-2.

Trompenaars, F. & Hampden-Turner, C. 1998). Riding the waves of culture: Understanding Diversity in Global Business (2nd ed.) New York, NY: McGraw-Hill.

Verne, J. (2012). *Leather Bound Classics.* San Diego, CA: Canterbury Classics/Baker.

White, B. J. (2014). *Boards that excel: Candid insights and practical advice for directors.* Oakland, CA: Berrett-Koehler.

The Author

The author of these essays is Samuel Dunn, currently Professor of Business at Northwest Nazarene University of Idaho. Dunn holds the PhD degree in Mathematics and the DBA degree in International Business.

Dunn served as Professor of Mathematics and Business, Dean, and Vice President for Academic Affairs at Seattle Pacific University, then Professor of Business and Mathematics and Vice President for Academic Affairs at Northwest Nazarene University. He is a long-time futurist, with several publications in futurist journals.

After a few years as a professor of mathematics, Dunn moved into academic administration. In that role he viewed himself as a business-person working in the second largest civilian industry in the United States, which is education. The essays in this book come from his experience as a management leader dealing with opportunities and challenges in a growth industry.

For fun Dunn likes to travel, read, and take Saturday tips with his wife, Lois. At the time of this writing he has been in 53 countries. The Dunns have two grown children; one is a forensic scientist serving in the United States and the other is a medical doctor serving in Asia.

69
Management
Tips
For Top Leaders

═══════════════════════

In this book you will find leadership insights garnered from 30 years of organizational experience. The author shares with you his observations and advice about methods that work and some that don't work. His careful advice and occasional admonitions will benefit you as provide leadership to for-profit and not-for-profit organizations.

www.ingramcontent.com/pod-product-compliance
Lightning Source LLC
Chambersburg PA
CBHW052109230326
41599CB00054B/5270